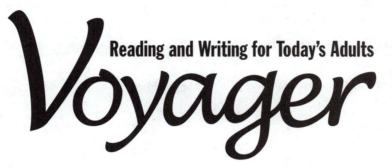

Reading and Writing for Today's Adults

Voyager

3

Sarah Chodera

Advisers to the Series

Mary Dunn Siedow
Director
North Carolina Literacy Resource Center
Raleigh, NC

Linda Thistlethwaite
Associate Director
The Central Illinois Adult Education Service Center
Western Illinois University
Macomb, IL

Reviewer

Mary Sattler
Student Group Coordinator
Project Learn
Akron, OH

New Readers Press

Acknowledgments

Anderson, Susan, "Arthur," TO OPEN YOUR MIND, Volume 5, Number 1, Winter 1995. Every effort has been made to contact the author for permission to reprint. If the author is located subsequent to publication, she is hereby entitled to due compensation.

Walker, Margaret, "Lineage" from FOR MY PEOPLE by Margaret Walker. Reprinted by permission of the author.

Zaret, Hy, "It Could Be a Wonderful World." Reprinted by permission.

ISBN 1-56420-153-8
Copyright © 1999
New Readers Press
U.S. Publishing Division of Laubach Literacy International
Box 131, Syracuse, New York 13210-0131

Printed in the United States of America
9 8 7 6 5 4 3

Director of Acquisitions and Development: Christina Jagger
Content Editor: Mary Hutchison
Developer: Learning Unlimited, Oak Park, IL
Developmental Editor: Pamela Bliss
Contributing Writer: Betsy Rubin
Photography: David Revette Photography, Inc.
Cover Designer: Gerald Russell
Designer: Kimbrly Koennecke
Artist: Linda Alden
Illustrator: Cheri Bladholm

Contents

Introduction

Welcome to New Readers Press's *Voyager 3*. In this book, you will build your skills in reading and writing. You will improve your understanding of what you read. You will also work with your listening and speaking skills.

This book has four units. Each unit is based on a theme that reflects our day-to-day lives. In *Voyager 3,* you will be exploring these themes:

▶ Great Expectations
▶ Across Generations
▶ Voices for Justice
▶ Express Yourself

Within each theme-based unit, you will find three lessons. Each lesson has the following features:

▶ **Before You Read:** a strategy to help you understand what you read
▶ **Key Words:** a preview of the harder words in the lesson
▶ **Reading:** a poem, song, story, biography, journal, speech, or review written by adults, for adults
▶ **After You Read:** questions and activities about the reading
▶ **Think About It:** a reading skill that will help you understand what you read
▶ **Write About It:** an activity to improve your writing skills

Eight lessons also have this feature:

▶ **Word Work:** strategies and skills to help you read and write better

We hope you enjoy exploring the themes and mastering the skills found in *Voyager 3*. We also invite you to continue your studies with the next book in our series, *Voyager 4.*

Student Interest Inventory

What is my educational goal?

_____

Check this side **BEFORE** you do this book.   Check this side **AFTER** you do this book.

Yes, I do	I need help	No, I don't	**What do I read?**	Yes, I do	I need help	No, I don't
			• instructions			
			• letters and other mail			
			• stories and poems			
			• newspapers and magazines			
			• material for my job			
			• books to my children			
			• other: _____			

Yes, I do	I need help	No, I don't	**When I read, I**	Yes, I do	I need help	No, I don't
			• use context clues to figure out new words			
			• break long words into smaller parts to figure them out			
			• use what I already know to help me understand what I read			
			• try to predict what is coming next as I read			
			• look for a theme in a poem			
			• recognize the main ideas and their supporting details			
			• pay attention to parts of the plot in stories			
			• am aware of the setting and characters in a story			
			• recognize that writers have different viewpoints about a subject			

Check this side **BEFORE** you do this book.

Check this side **AFTER** you do this book.

Yes, I do	I need help	No, I don't	I write or fill out	Yes, I do	I need help	No, I don't
			• lists			
			• notes and messages			
			• letters			
			• songs and poems			
			• stories			
			• journal entries			
			• forms and applications			
			• descriptions of characters I read about			
			• results of an interview			
			• reviews of movies and TV shows			
			• other: _____			

Yes, I can	I need help	No, I can't	When I write, I can	Yes, I can	I need help	No, I can't
			• think of good ideas			
			• organize my ideas			
			• express myself clearly so others understand what I mean			
			• use details to support my main ideas			
			• write compound and complex sentences			
			• capitalize and punctuate sentences correctly			
			• recognize fragments and fix them			

Skills Preview

This preview will give you an idea of what you will do in this book. Before you begin Unit 1, complete as much of this preview as you can. Share your work with your instructor.

Reading Skills Preview

Read each passage and answer the questions that follow.

A Family Story

When Leo Kent turned 42, his life changed. Before Leo even took a bite of his birthday dinner, his wife, Julie, said, "Leo, I have something to tell you. You're going to be a father."

Leo's world turned upside down. He had thought they could not have kids. Now, after 15 years of marriage, they would have to prepare for one. Leo hugged Julie, but he began to think. How would a baby change his life? Could he adjust to the changes? Was he too old? Did he even want a child anymore?

A few nights later, Leo found Julie crying. "What's the matter, honey?" Leo asked.

Julie looked him straight in the eye. "I don't think you want this baby," she said. Leo stared at his wife. Suddenly he knew the truth. He was scared, but he did want this child. Leo took a deep breath. He was ready to tell Julie how he felt.

Choose the best answer for each question.

1. What problem does Leo face in this story?
    (1) saving his marriage
    (2) becoming a father unexpectedly
    (3) understanding his wife

2. Because of all the questions Leo asks himself, you can infer that he feels

   (1) happy   (2) angry   (3) worried

3. Julie is the kind of person who

   (1) is direct and honest   (2) keeps her feelings to herself   (3) hates surprises

We Shall Overcome

We shall overcome, we shall overcome,
We shall overcome some day.
Oh, deep in my heart I do believe
We shall overcome some day.

We'll go hand in hand,
We'll go hand in hand,
We'll go hand in hand some day.
Oh, deep in my heart I do believe
We'll go hand in hand some day.

We are not afraid, we are not afraid,
We are not afraid today.
Oh, deep in my heart I do believe
We are not afraid today.

We shall overcome, we shall overcome,
We shall overcome some day.
Oh, deep in my heart I do believe
We shall overcome some day.

Choose the best answer for each question.

4. What is the theme of this song?
   (1) Hardship and pain are in all people's lives.
   (2) Working together and believing deeply will lead to change.
   (3) Everyone should work to help the poor.

5. Which of these people would most likely sing this song?
   (1) the leader of a nation
   (2) a civil rights worker
   (3) the president of a company

Write About It

On a separate paper, write about the topic below. Use the revising checklist on page 10 to check your draft. Give your draft to your instructor for feedback.

Topic: Write about a great expectation you have, for yourself or for someone you love. Explain why you have this dream.

Skills Preview Answers

Reading Skills Preview

1. (2)
2. (3)
3. (1)
4. (2)
5. (2)

Revising Checklist

Revise your draft. Check that your draft

_____ includes your important ideas

_____ has details to explain what you mean

_____ is clear and easy to understand

Make changes on your first draft to improve your writing. Then share your draft with your instructor.

Skills Chart

The questions in the Skills Preview assess students' familiarity with the following skills: *Voyager: Reading and Writing for Today's Adults™ Voyager 3*

Question	Reading Skill
1	understand plot
2	make inferences
3	understand character
4	find the theme
5	identify viewpoint

Unit 1 Great Expectations

When you think about the future, what kind of expectations do you have? Do you expect good things to happen? Do you expect to find a job or get a better job? Do you plan to earn a GED? Do you want to travel?

You might have great expectations for yourself, for your family, or for the world. It is important to have great expectations—and work to reach them. Great expectations can help direct your life. They can give your life more meaning.

▶ **Be an Active Reader**

As you read the selections in this unit

• Put a question mark (?) by things you do not understand.
• <u>Underline</u> words you do not know. Try to use context clues to figure them out.

Lesson 1

LEARNING GOALS

Strategy: Use your experience to help you understand what you read
Reading: Read the words to a song
Skill: Find the theme
Writing: Write a song

Before You Read

"It Could Be a Wonderful World" is a song that was written soon after World War II ended. The song tells the writer's ideas about how the world could be a better place.

Before you read "It Could Be a Wonderful World," think about ways you feel the world could be better. Complete each sentence below with an idea of your own.

The world would be a better place if

every worker _____

every homeless person _____

every child _____

Key Words Read each sentence. Do you know the underlined words?
- Do we think of each other as <u>neighbors</u>, friends, and family?
- Do people know that true <u>brotherhood</u> means treating each other like family?
- Are rich people <u>content</u> with all their belongings?

Use the Strategy

To help you understand this song, think about the world we live in. What is good about it? What is bad about it? Think about how your experiences relate to the ideas in the song.

It Could Be a Wonderful World

Hy Zaret and Lou Singer

If each little kid could have fresh milk each day,
If each working man had enough time to play,
If each homeless soul had a good place to stay,
It could be a wonderful world.

If we could consider each other
A neighbor, a friend, or a brother,
It could be a wonderful, wonderful world,
It could be a wonderful world.

If there were no poor and the rich were content,
If strangers were welcome wherever they went,
If each of us knew what true brotherhood meant,
It could be a wonderful world.

If we could consider each other
A neighbor, a friend, or a brother,
It could be a wonderful, wonderful world,
It could be a wonderful world.

Check-in

How do the ideas in the song relate to your ideas about how the world could be better? Compare the ideas you wrote in "Before You Read" on page 12 with the ideas in the song.

After You Read

A. Did the Song Make Sense? Reread sections you marked with a question mark (?). Do they make sense now? If not, discuss them with a partner or your instructor.

B. Build Your Vocabulary Look at the words you <u>underlined</u>. Can you figure them out now? If not, find out what they are. Add them to your word bank.

C. Answer These Questions

1. Write the basic need that each idea describes.

   a. "If each little kid could have fresh milk each day"

   This idea describes everyone's need for _____.

   b. "If each working man had enough time to play"

   This idea describes everyone's need to _____.

   c. "If each homeless soul had a good place to stay"

   This idea describes everyone's need for _____.

2. Which is the topic of the song?
   (1) wishes for the world
   (2) wonders of the world
   (3) people in the world

3. If the songwriter could act on his ideas, what might he do? Check each action he might take.

   _____ make a new start by changing jobs

   _____ start a free food program for children

   _____ open a shelter for the homeless

   ▶ **Talk About It**

   Discuss the questions below with a partner or small group. If you like, write a response.

   Which of the problems in the song do you think is most important? Why? What can be done to help solve this problem?

Think About It: Find the Theme

Many pieces of writing have themes. A **theme** is the message about life that a writer wants to tell. For example, the theme of "It Could Be a Wonderful World" is how the world could be a kinder, fairer place.

Often themes are based on topics that are important parts of life, such as

love	friendship	family	justice
nature	religion	death	growing older

When you read a piece of writing, look for its theme. To find the theme, ask yourself these two questions:

1. What is the topic?

2. What is the writer saying about this topic? This message is the theme.

Below on the left is a list of topics. On the right is one possible theme for each topic. Match each theme with its topic. The first one is done for you.

Topic

   _c_   **1.** love

        2. parenthood

        3. working

        4. growing older

        5. death

Theme

a. coping with the aging process

b. feelings when a life ends

c. the caring and respect between a husband and wife

d. the challenge of being a single mother

e. the problems and rewards of a job

Did you match these themes and topics?

2. d
3. e
4. a
5. b

Practice Read each short selection. Then answer the questions about its topic and theme.

A. Thousands of people in this country are homeless. Every day, these people may face very cold or very hot weather. They lack food and a place to sleep. Many of the homeless feel the stares of other people. They may remember a better time in their lives. The hours pass.

  1. What is the topic? _____

  2. Which is the theme, or message, about the topic?
     (1) ways people can help the homeless
     (2) the pain and hardship of homelessness
     (3) the large numbers of homeless

B. Tony Ori could not take it any longer. He turned the TV news off. He was tired of seeing the faces of hungry children. He was tired of hearing their cries. Right then Tony made a decision. Maybe he could not solve the world's hunger problem. But he could help the hungry people in his own town. Tony decided he would start a food collection. Grocery stores and restaurants could give extra food. People could donate food. Tony made himself a promise. By this time next year, not one person in his hometown would go to bed hungry.

  3. What is the topic? _____

  4. Which is the theme, or message, about the topic?
     (1) who goes to bed hungry
     (2) why people are hungry
     (3) how one man decided to help the hungry

Write About It: Write a Song

You have read a songwriter's ideas about making the world better. Now work with one or more partners to finish a song with your ideas.

First read the song "It Could Be a Wonderful World" out loud. Listen for the words that rhyme (like *day, play, stay*). Next read the song again. Clap along with the rhythm, or the beat, of the words.

A. **Prewrite** Read each line in the song below. Think of words and phrases to complete the line. Have one person write down all the ideas on a separate sheet.

B. **Write** Decide if you want your song to rhyme. Choose the words that fit the lines best and write them on the lines.

Our World Could Be a Better Place ▬▬▬

If every man and woman had _____,

If every person knew _____,

If people worked together for _____,

Our world could be a better place.

If no one _____,

If we could all just _____,

Our world could be a fairer place

Our world would be a better place.

Read your song out loud. What kind of music would you pick for your words? Do you know a tune that they would fit? If not, try to make up a tune to fit them.

▶ **Hold on to this work.** You may use it again at the end of this unit.

Lesson 2

LEARNING GOALS

Strategy: Predict the features of a story
Reading: Read a story
Skill: Understand the plot
Writing: Write a story
Word Work: Use context clues to figure out word meaning

Before You Read

"The New Boss" is a story about a woman with a new job. She is in charge of an auto assembly line.

Before you read "The New Boss," think about stories you have read. Check each feature you expect to find in a story.

_____ characters (people in the story)

_____ a setting (the time and place)

_____ facts about the world

_____ a conflict or problem

_____ a climax, or turning point in the action

_____ an ending (happy or sad)

_____ what the writer thinks about the story

Key Words Read each sentence. Do you know the underlined words?

- Kim was <u>qualified</u> for the job because of her <u>experience</u>.
- When workers feel <u>resentful</u>, they feel anger and ill will.
- Kim was given <u>authority</u> to lead the assembly line.

▶ **Use the Strategy**

"The New Boss" is a story about Kim Washington. She is starting a new job as the boss on an assembly line. To understand the story better, watch for these story features—characters, the setting, a conflict, a climax, and an ending.

The New Boss

Kim Washington walked by row after row of workers. Today was her third day in this factory. She was manager of the 40 people on this auto assembly line. Kim was qualified for this job. She had worked on a line for 10 years. Kim had high expectations for herself. She wanted to be a good and fair boss. She also had high expectations for the workers on the line. She wanted them to produce more cars faster and better, and help cut costs.

These goals would not be easy to meet. Many of the workers were resentful of her authority. They were men with years of experience. Kim knew that they did not think she was qualified. She also knew that some of the men did not want to work for a woman boss.

Check-in ▶ Think about the story so far. Who is the main character? What conflict do you think will develop?

As Kim walked the floor, she saw a man about to bolt a car frame with a rivet gun. He was holding the gun the wrong way. Kim knew how easily a rivet gun could get out of control. She had seen workers lose fingers before.

Kim called out, "Hey, let's follow the rules here. I don't want to see ten thousand pounds of pressure nail your finger instead of that rivet."

At first the man seemed to ignore her. Then he whirled around. The expression on his face was angry and resentful. His tag read "Todd Walker."

"Look, lady," Todd said loudly. "I don't expect any help from you. If you want to know what we think, I'll tell you. We don't want you here. What do you know about working a line? There are a dozen men here more qualified than you. We don't want a woman boss."

◀ **Check-in**

Notice how tension is rising. The action is building to a climax. What do you think Kim might do next?

Kim knew that everyone on the line was watching and listening. She chose her words carefully.

"Todd, I know more than you think about working a line. I did it for ten years. In time, you'll find out that I expect a lot from myself and from you. When I know how much each worker can do, I'll give him the authority he deserves. For now, if you see something happening that looks wrong or dangerous, you don't need my OK to shut down the line. I give every worker on my line that authority."

Todd Walker looked surprised. Kim continued.

"Now, you seem to have a problem with my being a woman. Well, I really can't help that. But that has nothing to do with whether I'm a qualified manager."

Todd Walker stared at Kim, then nodded slightly. He turned back to the line. A few of the men standing near him smiled or nodded at Kim. Kim said, "Let's get back to work. We have goals to meet."

▶ **Final Check-in**

Look at the list of features you checked on page 18. Did you find the features you expected to find in the story? How did you feel about the ending?

After You Read

A. Did the Story Make Sense? Reread sections you marked with a question mark (?). Do they make sense now? If not, discuss them with a partner or your instructor.

B. Build Your Vocabulary Look at the words you <u>underlined</u>. Can you figure them out now? If not, find out what they are. Add them to your word bank.

C. Answer These Questions

1. Name the two main characters in the story. Then write a few words to tell about the other story features.

   a. Characters (people): _____ and _____

   b. Setting (place): _____

   c. Conflict (problem): _____

   d. Ending: _____

2. How does Kim handle Todd Walker?
   (1) She responds calmly to his anger.
   (2) She walks away to avoid a fight.
   (3) She argues with him.

3. How would Kim likely act toward a lazy worker?
   (1) fire him right away
   (2) talk to him about his work
   (3) pretend there was not a problem

▶ **Talk About It**

Discuss the question below with a partner or small group.
If you like, write a response.

Do you think Kim will meet her expectations and be a good boss?
Why or why not?

Think About It: Understand the Plot

Every story has a plot. A **plot** is the action or series of events in the story. The plot usually has three parts:

1. The **rising action** introduces the characters and the main problem or conflict.

2. The **climax** is the turning point in the action. It is the point when you feel the most tense because you know something important is about to happen. The climax usually occurs near the end of the story.

3. The **falling action** tells what happens after the climax. The plot draws quickly to a close.

Here is the plot of "The New Boss:"

1. **Rising action:** Kim Washington walks down the assembly line. She thinks about her new job. She sees Todd Walker holding a tool the wrong way. She warns him. Todd becomes angry and challenges her authority.

2. **Climax:** Everyone watches and listens. Kim carefully decides what to say to Todd.

3. **Falling Action:** Kim responds to Todd. He calms down. Work continues.

The plot map below shows how you can picture a plot. It is filled in with the three parts of "The New Boss."

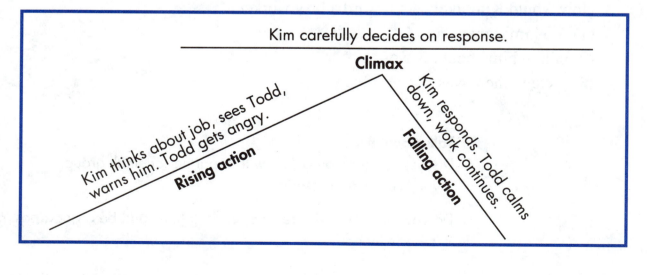

Practice Each story below has its own plot. On the lines, fill in the rising action, the climax, and the falling action. The first one is started for you.

1. Todd Walker went back to his work. Suddenly Bill Tyler spoke to him loudly. "That's the new boss," he said. "You should show her some respect." Todd did not like Bill's comments. He pushed Bill. Bill pushed him back. Just then the workers nearby moved in and broke up the fight. "We don't want any more trouble," one said. Everyone went back to work.

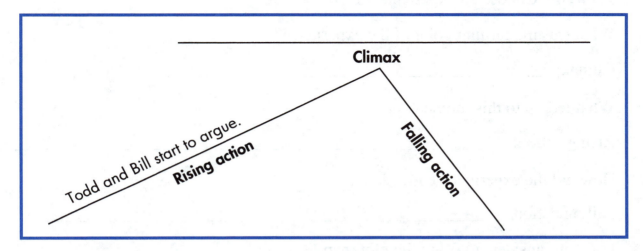

2. A few weeks later, Todd saw a new worker about to use a rivet gun. "Hey!" Todd shouted. "Be careful! You're going to lose control of that gun!" The worker did not hear Todd. Todd ran to the controls. He shut down the line. Kim Washington ran from the other side of the plant. Todd explained what happened. Kim thanked Todd for his quick thinking.

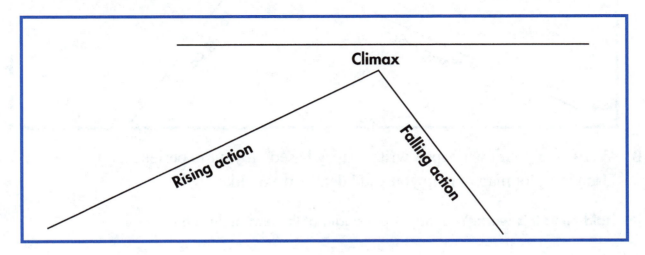

Write About It: Write a Story

Authors often base their plots on things that happen in real life. Think about your own life. Which of these experiences have you had?

an argument   a robbery   getting married
an accident   getting a job   having a child

Write a story about one of these experiences or another experience in your life.

A. Prewrite Choose an experience to write about.

What was the turning point of the experience?

Climax: _____

What led up to this moment?

Rising action: _____

How did the experience end?

Falling action: _____

Use your answers to fill in the plot map.

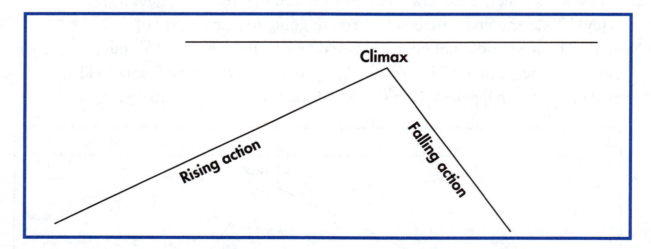

B. Write On your own paper, write a story based on your experience. Use your plot map to help you. Add details if you like.

▶ **Hold on to this work.** You may use it again at the end of this unit.

Word Work: Using Context Clues to Figure Out Word Meaning

When you come to an unfamiliar word in your reading, the words and sentences around it can provide hints. These hints are called **context clues.** Context clues can be used to figure out the meaning and the pronunciation of unfamiliar words. Here are some tips for using context clues.

Tip 1 Look for clues to the meaning *after* the hard word. Look later in the same sentence or in later sentences in the paragraph.

• Kim was qualified for the job because she had *years of experience.*

If you did not know the meaning of *qualified,* the context clue, *years of experience,* tells you what *qualified* means.

Tip 2 Look for a definition of the hard word in the same sentence or the next sentence.

• Kim knew how to restrain, or *hold back,* her feelings.
• Kim knew how to restrain her feelings. She *held them back.*

Tip 3 Look for examples to help explain the hard word.

• Kim wouldn't show strong emotions, *like anger,* at work.

Practice Look for context clues in the sentences below. Then choose the meaning of each underlined word.

1. Kim can usually <u>identify</u>, or spot, unhappy workers on the line.
   (1) find or notice (2) help (3) talk to

2. Men on the line <u>assemble</u>, or put together, cars.
   (1) design (2) put together (3) fix

3. Every worker must follow safety <u>guidelines</u>, such as wearing goggles and steel-toe shoes.
   (1) lines on the floor (2) rules (3) signs

Lesson 3

LEARNING GOALS

Strategy: Understand how another person feels
Reading: Read a biography
Skill: Find the main idea and details
Writing: Write a paragraph
Word Work: Recognizing words

Before You Read

"Shaq Measures Up" tells about the early life of basketball star Shaquille [sha KEEL] O'Neal. It is a short biography of his early years. A biography is a piece of writing that tells about a real person's life.

Before you read about Shaq, think about your own life. Think about a time when you felt under pressure to do something well. Answer these questions about that time:

What was the reason you felt pressure?

_____

How did you handle the pressure?

_____

Key Words Read each sentence. Do you know the underlined words?
- Shaquille O'Neal's first coach said Shaq could become a <u>professional</u> player.
- Shaquille's father was a <u>sergeant</u> in the army.
- As a teenager, Shaquille needed to learn <u>discipline</u>.
- Shaquille scored an <u>average</u> of 24 points a game.

► **Use the Strategy**

To help you understand Shaquille O'Neal's biography, put yourself in his shoes. What kind of pressures would you feel? Notice how Shaquille faced new pressures at each stage of his life.

Shaq Measures Up

Shaquille O'Neal was born on March 6, 1972. His parents called him Shaquille, which means "little one." But by the time Shaquille was 20, he was known around the country as "Shaq" or "Shaq Attack." He had become a basketball star. His success did not come easy. All his life, Shaq worked hard to meet the high expectations of himself and others.

When Shaq was 13, a coach and his father set different goals for him. The coach, Dale Brown, saw Shaq play at a basketball clinic. He thought Shaq could go on to play professional ball.

Shaq's father had other ideas. He said, "Coach Brown, I don't mean to be rude, but I'm not all that interested about basketball." Shaq's father thought African Americans should work to be leaders, such as heads of corporations and generals.

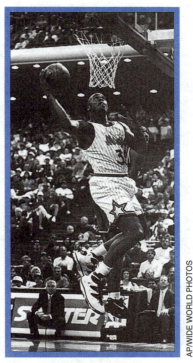

SHAQUILLE O'NEAL

AP/WIDE WORLD PHOTOS

Shaq's father was a sergeant in the U.S. Army. The family moved from army post to army post. When Shaq caused problems, his father was strict. "I was a bad kid," Shaq once said. But his father steered his son the right way. Shaq said his dad "put it to me a lot. I have a lot of discipline now, and if it wasn't for him, I don't know where I'd be."

Check-in ► Think about Shaq's life so far. How would you feel if a coach and your father set different goals for you?

Because Shaq was so good in high school basketball, he was expected to be a great college player. Dale Brown, the coach for Louisiana State University, got him to play there. Shaq played well his first two years. But in his third year, he began to have trouble. He didn't score as many points. His mind did not seem to be on the game. People said he was just waiting to get out of college. They said he wanted to make money as a professional player.

◀ **Check-in**

How would you feel if you were a good player who stopped playing well? How would you feel if people said you were just thinking of money?

Shaq turned to his family for advice. Shaq's father told him he was playing "too nice." Shaq's grandmother told him to play as he used to, "yelling, dunking, hanging on the rim, and diving on the floor."

Shaq turned his game around. He finished his third year of college with an average of 24.1 points a game. He scored more each game than most other players. Shaq was ready for the NBA.

In 1992, the Orlando Magic made Shaq the number one pick in the NBA draft. They agreed to pay him $40 million for seven years. As a professional, Shaq had to play against stars like Michael Jordan and Patrick Ewing. Would Shaq be good enough?

In many games his first year, Shaq led his team in scoring, rebounding, and blocking shots. He started in the NBA All-Star Game. He was named NBA Rookie of the Year. Once again, Shaq had measured up.

▶ **Final Check-in**

Compare the pressures Shaq felt with the pressure you felt and wrote about in "Before You Read" on page 26.
How was your experience the same? How was it different?

After You Read

A. Did the Reading Make Sense? Reread sections you marked with a question mark (?). Do they make sense now? If not, discuss them with a partner or your instructor.

B. Build Your Vocabulary Look at the words you <u>underlined</u>. Can you figure them out now? If not, find out what they are. Add them to your word bank.

C. Answer These Questions

1. How do you think Shaq felt:

   a. during his third year in college? _____

   b. after his first year in the NBA? _____

2. Give one example of how Shaq lived up to high expectations.

   _____

3. "If it wasn't for my father, I don't know where I'd be." What does Shaq mean by this?
   (1) Without his dad's help, Shaq's life would be very different.
   (2) Shaq's dad told Shaq he should play in the NBA.
   (3) If Shaq did not have a father, Shaq would be living someplace else.

 Talk About It
Discuss the questions below with a partner or small group.
If you like, write a response.

Do people expect too much of athletes? How did Shaq seem to handle the pressure of people's expectations?

Think About It: Find the Main Idea and Details

A **paragraph** is a group of sentences with one main idea and several supporting details. The **main idea** is the most important point. The **supporting details** explain, or support, the main idea. In this paragraph, the main idea is in heavy type:

> **All his life, Shaq has worked to meet high expectations.** He met his dad's expectations when he learned discipline. He met fans' expectations when he began playing well again in college. But that is not all. Shaq met everyone's expectations when he was named the NBA Rookie of the Year.

These details in the paragraph support the main idea:
- Shaq met his dad's expectations by learning discipline.
- Shaq met fans' expectations by playing well again.

What is a third detail that supports the main idea?

_____

Did you write that Shaq met everyone's expectations by being named the NBA Rookie of the Year? Then you were right.

Picture a main idea and supporting details like this:

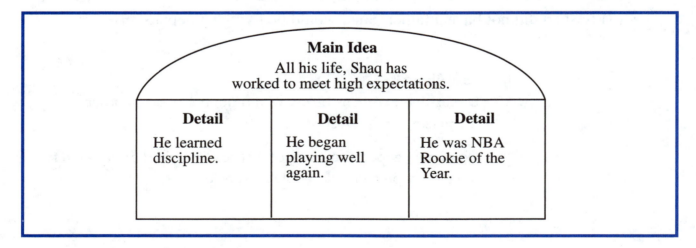

Main Idea
All his life, Shaq has
worked to meet high expectations.

Detail	**Detail**	**Detail**
He learned discipline.	He began playing well again.	He was NBA Rookie of the Year.

Practice Read each paragraph. Write its main idea and supporting details.
The first one is started for you.

1. Professional athletes may not meet fans' high expectations for
   many reasons. They may earn so much money that they lose
   their edge as athletes. They may be tempted by drugs. They
   may not be able to handle the pressure of playing before
   millions of people.

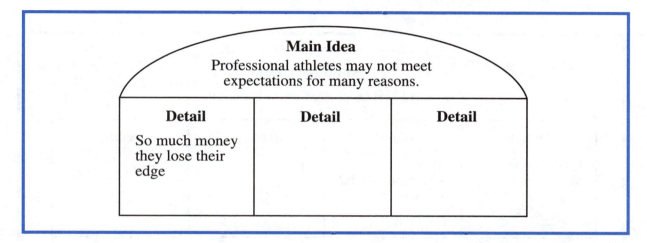

2. Parents often have high expectations for their children. They
   expect their children to be honest and to follow the rules.
   They expect their children to get along with others. They
   expect their children to do their best. Sometimes parents
   expect their children to become what the parents wanted
   to be but could not be.

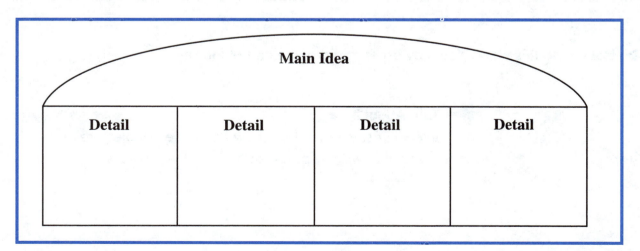

Write About It: Write a Paragraph

Sometimes we feel pressure when we try to meet expectations. Everyone handles pressure in a different way. You read how Shaquille O'Neal turned to his family for advice. Now write a paragraph about how you handle pressure.

A. Prewrite Think about things you do to handle pressure. Do you listen to music? If so, what kind? Do you talk to someone? If so, who? Fill in details in the boxes below.

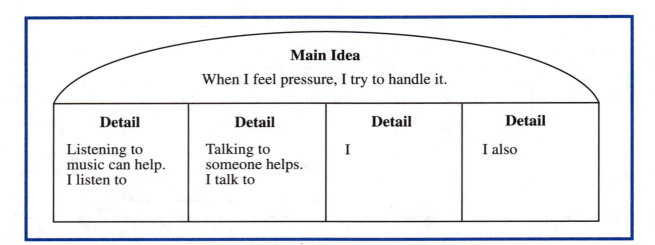

Main Idea

When I feel pressure, I try to handle it.

Detail	Detail	Detail	Detail
Listening to music can help. I listen to	Talking to someone helps. I talk to	I	I also

B. Write Complete this paragraph on your own paper. Use the details you wrote in the chart.

When I feel pressure, I try to handle it. I _____

_____

▶ **Hold on to this work.** You may use it again at the end of this unit.

 **Talk About It**

Interview someone about how he or she handles pressure. If you like, write a paragraph about the answers.

Word Work: Recognizing Words

One good strategy for figuring out words you don't know when you are reading is to use context clues. If the unknown word is a long word, there are three more strategies you can use along with context clues:

- You can divide a **compound word** into its smaller words.
- You can divide words with **roots, prefixes,** and **suffixes** into those parts.
- You can divide words with two or more **syllables** into those parts.

In the Word Work lessons in the rest of this book, you will learn how to use these strategies.

▶ **Remember:** When trying to figure out an unknown word, if you say a word you don't recognize, try another pronunciation. You will probably recognize the word when you get it right. Then check your guess in the context of the reading or in a dictionary.

Dividing Compound Words

A **compound word** is a word made up of two or more words:

any|one   basket|ball   grand|mother

Tip   If you are reading and come to a word that you don't recognize, see if it has smaller words in it that you do recognize.

Practice Draw a line between the smaller words in each compound word. Then write the words that make up the compound word. The first one is started for you.

1. under|stand   _____under_____   _____

2. afternoon   _____   _____

3. classroom   _____   _____

4. thumbnail   _____   _____

5. everywhere   _____   _____

▶ Writing Skills Mini-Lesson: Compound Sentences

A **compound sentence** has two or more complete thoughts joined by a connecting word like one of these: *and, but, so, or.* To write a compound sentence, follow these rules:

1. **Make each part of the sentence a *complete thought.*** Include a **subject** (who or what the sentence is about) and a **verb** (what the subject does or is).

     S V   S   V

   I have a plan for my future, and **nobody will stop** me.

2. **Use the correct connecting word.**
   - *and* for related ideas
   - *but* for contrasting ideas
   - *so* for one idea that causes another
   - *or* for two choices

3. **Use a *comma* before the connecting word.**
   - I am older than the other students, **but** I don't mind.
   - My sons are now in school, **so** I have more time to study.
   - I can take a GED class, **or** I can study on my own.

Practice On your own paper, write five compound sentences about your future plans or dreams. Include a subject and verb in each part of the sentence. Use the sentence parts below or some of your own.

1. I want to get a better job, so _____

2. _____ so I will study hard.

3. It may be difficult, but _____

4. _____ and I will work to meet this goal.

5. I will _____ or I will _____

Unit 1 Review

Reading Review

This reading is about great expectations. Read it and then answer the questions.

High Hopes

For Maria Diaz, the day was dragging by. Maria was an aide in a law office. For the past year, she had worked hard, hoping to become office manager. She had done her job well, as she always did. She had also stayed late and had taken on extra projects. Today the new office manager would be named. Maria hoped the job would be hers.

As Maria worked, she thought about what the extra money would mean for her family. The minutes ticked by. She began to feel nervous. Then at 3:30, Maria's phone rang. It was her boss, Mr. Greeley. He asked Maria to come to his office. Maria walked in and sat down in front of the large desk. Mr. Greeley studied her for a moment. Then he spoke. "As you know, Ms. Diaz, we've been looking for a new office manager." Then he smiled and said, "I'm happy to tell you we'd like to offer you the job."

Maria smiled with pride and relief. "Thank you, Mr. Greeley. I'll do the best job I know how," she said as she stood and shook his hand. Back at her desk, Maria called her husband with the good news.

Choose the best answer for each question.

1. What is the theme of this story?
   (1) Good workers get the best jobs.
   (2) Hard work can pay off.
   (3) Time drags when you are waiting.

2. What was the climax, or turning point of the story?
   (1) Maria was thinking about earning extra money.
   (2) Mr. Greeley offered Maria the office manager's job.
   (3) Maria called her husband.

3. What events led to Maria's getting the job of office manager?
   (1) Mr. Greeley told Maria she would be made office manager at the end of a year, and she was.
   (2) Maria needed extra money for her family, so she called Mr. Greeley and asked him for a better job.
   (3) Maria set a high goal, stayed late, and took on extra projects.

Writing Process

In Unit 1, you wrote three first drafts. Choose the piece that you would like to work with more. You will revise, edit, and make a final copy of this draft.

_____ your song about your hopes for the world (page 17)
_____ your story about an experience you had (page 24)
_____ your paragraph about handling pressure (page 32)

Find the first draft you chose. Then turn to page 128 in this book. Follow steps 3, 4, and 5 in the Writing Process to create a final draft.

As you revise, check your draft for this specific point:

Song: Does your song make your ideas and hopes for the world clear?

Story: Does the plot have rising action, climax, and falling action, in that order?

Paragraph: Does your paragraph contain supporting details that tell how you handle pressure?

Unit 2 Across Generations

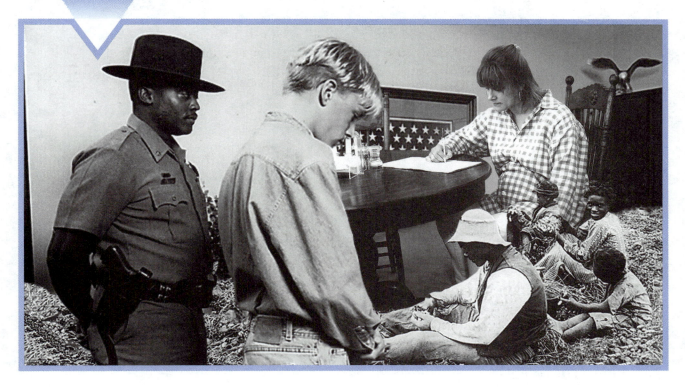

Every 20 or 25 years, a new generation is born. Your parents are one generation. You belong to another generation. If you have children, they are part of a third generation.

Each generation is different from the one before it and the one after it. For example, each generation has its own

- leaders
- events
- music
- clothing and hairstyles
- inventions
- lifestyles

Yet different generations also share many things. People in each generation love and hope. They work and play. And they live and learn. Different generations can share their thoughts with and learn from each other.

Before you start Unit 2, think of the people in your life. How are the people from different generations alike? How are they different?

▶ **Be an Active Reader**

As you read the selections in this unit
- Put a question mark (?) by things you do not understand.
- <u>Underline</u> words you do not know. Try to use context clues to figure them out.

Lesson 4

LEARNING GOALS

Strategy: Use your experience to understand what you read
Reading: Read a poem
Skill: Find the theme
Writing: Write a poem

Before You Read

The line of people in past generations of a family—great-grandparents, grandparents, and parents—is called a person's lineage [LIN ee ij]. In this lesson, you will read a poem called "Lineage." In the poem, Margaret Walker writes about her grandmothers. She tells how hard their lives were.

Before you read "Lineage," think about your own family and its past. What kind of life did past generations in your family have? Mark each statement **True** or **False.**

True	False	
_____	_____	Past generations in my family had a hard life.
_____	_____	Relationships between men and women were different in my family long ago.
_____	_____	Past generations in my family were more in touch with nature and the land than my generation is.
_____	_____	Past generations cared more about the family than my generation does.

Key Words Read each sentence. Do you know the underlined words?

- My grandmothers' <u>sturdiness</u> gave them the strength to work in the fields.
- The grandmothers have many <u>memories</u> of the past.

▶ **Use the Strategy**

In the poem "Lineage," the poet describes her grandmothers. To help you understand the poem, think about older relatives you know well. Are they like the grandmothers in the poem? How?

Lineage

Margaret Walker

CORBIS/BETTMANN

My grandmothers were strong.
They followed plows and bent to toil.
They moved through fields sowing seed.
They touched earth and grain grew.
They were full of sturdiness and singing.
My grandmothers were strong.

My grandmothers are full of memories
Smelling of soap and onions and wet clay
With veins rolling roughly over quick hands
They have many clean words to say.
My grandmothers were strong.
Why am I not as they?

▶ **Check-in**

How do the grandmothers in the poem compare with your older relatives? Look at the statements you checked as True on page 38. How do those statements compare with the ideas in the poem?

After You Read

A. Did the Poem Make Sense? Reread sections you marked with a question mark (?). Do they make sense now? If not, discuss them with a partner or your instructor.

B. Build Your Vocabulary Look at the words you underlined. Can you figure them out now? If not, find out what they are. Add them to your word bank.

C. Answer These Questions

1. Choose the underlined term you agree with. Then finish the sentence.

   My grandmothers <u>were</u> or <u>were not</u> like the grandmothers in the poem

   because _____

2. Check each word or phrase below that describes the grandmothers in the poem.

   _____ sturdy   _____ quick   _____ powerful

   _____ able   _____ weak   _____ sickly

   _____ lazy   _____ forgetful   _____ full of energy

3. What does the poet mean when she says, "Why am I not as they?"
   (1) She is not as strong a person as her grandmothers.
   (2) She does not think her grandmothers loved her.
   (3) She does not look like a member of the family.

▶ **Talk About It**
Discuss the questions below with a partner or small group. If you like, write a response.

How is your life easier than your grandparents' lives? How is it harder?

Think About It: Find the Theme

You have learned that most pieces of writing have a theme. A **theme** is the message about life that the writer is telling you.

To find the theme, first ask, "What is the general topic of the piece?" In the poem "Lineage," each stanza, or group of lines, starts with the words "My grandmothers." Each line talks about grandmothers. So the topic is grandmothers.

Then ask yourself, "What is the writer saying about the topic?" In "Lineage," the poet says these things:

- Her grandmothers were strong.
- They had sturdiness.
- They worked hard.
- They are full of memories and singing.

So the theme of "Lineage" is grandmothers being strong and full of memories.

Read this paragraph. Find its theme by completing the sentences that follow.

> Every generation enjoys new inventions. When my grandfather was a boy in the 1920s, the automobile was a new invention. When my father was a boy in the 1950s, television was new. The big change in my life has been the computer. I use a computer every day at work, and my kids learn from computers at school.

The topic of the paragraph is new _____

The author writes that new inventions are enjoyed by every

_____

The topic of the paragraph is new inventions. The author writes that new inventions are enjoyed by every generation. That is the theme.

Practice Read each passage and answer the questions.

A. Grandparents are an important link to the past. They can tell you what life was like 50 or 60 years ago. They can tell you about World War II, about swing music, and about how men and women used to meet and date. Grandchildren should ask them questions so that the past is not lost. I hope my own grandchildren will ask me about my life someday. I will tell them about the war in Bosnia, rap music, and how I met my wife.

1. What is the topic? _____

2. What is the theme? _____

B. Single Father

Some days I think
I cannot do this alone.

Then my child looks up at me
With large eyes and love.
Single father. Single father.
The words sound so alone.
But I am not alone. I'm with him.

3. What is the topic? _____

4. What is the theme? _____

Write About It: Write a Poem

The poem "Lineage" describes the poet's grandmothers. Write a poem about members of your own family.

A. Prewrite Think about your grandparents, your parents, yourself, and other members of your family. List some names that come to mind. Also note things you remember about your family members.

My grandparents _____

They _____

_____

My parents _____

They _____

_____

I _____

I _____

_____

My family _____

We _____

_____

B. Write On your own paper, write a poem called "Family." Choose your best ideas from above.

Read your poem out loud. What feelings do you have when you hear it? If you like, share it with a friend.

▶ **Hold on to this work.** You may use it again at the end of this unit.

Lesson 5

LEARNING GOALS

Strategy: Predict what you might read about
Reading: Read a journal
Skill: Draw conclusions
Writing: Write a journal entry
Word Work: Prefixes and roots

Before You Read

"A Mother's Gift" is from a journal written by a young woman named Tina. She is expecting her first baby.

In a journal, a person writes what he or she is thinking and feeling. Before you read Tina's journal, think about what she might have written in it. Check each item you expect to read about in Tina's journal.

_____ her feelings about becoming a mother

_____ her relationship with the baby's father

_____ how her body is changing

List other things you think you might read about in Tina's journal.

_____

_____

Key Words Read each sentence. Do you know the underlined words?
- I went to a program for people with an <u>addiction</u> to <u>alcohol</u>.
- Staying away from alcohol is the only way to be a <u>responsible</u> mother.
- Your father <u>suspected</u> that I had a drinking problem.
- He <u>confronted</u> me with the fact that I drank.

▶ **Use the Strategy**

To help you understand Tina's journal, notice what she is writing about. See if you can predict what will happen. See if you can predict what she will write about next.

A Mother's Gift

Monday, March 3

My name is Tina. I am writing this journal as a gift for you, my baby boy. In four months, you will come into this world. Your father and I will name you David. In Hebrew, this name means "beloved one." I will write down my thoughts and experiences during the first years of your life. Someday I will give you this journal.

David, your birthplace will be Los Angeles, California. When you are born, you will come home to live with your father and me. We got married eight months ago, but we have been together three years. We know that a baby can be hard on a relationship. We will do everything we can to make it work.

Thursday, March 6

David, today I began painting your bedroom light blue. While I worked, I thought about the last year of my life. Almost one year ago, I went to a program for people who have an addiction to alcohol. Very few people know this.

Check-in ▶ What important information did Tina just reveal? What do you think she will talk about next?

I have not had a drink for 10 months. I am proud of this. It has not been easy. If I had become pregnant before I faced my addiction, I don't know what would have happened to us.

David, I believe that I will stay sober. I know that is the only way to be a responsible mother.

Monday, March 10

Today was a special day. Your father and I were at the store. We were looking at a playpen when I felt you kick for the first time. You can kick hard! I said, "Honey, I think this baby will be strong and stubborn like you." Then I added, "And thank goodness you are."

◀ **Check-in**

What comment did Tina just make? What do you think she will tell next?

I started drinking as a young teen. Your father never knew I had a problem until we moved in together. Then he suspected right away. When he confronted me, I lied. I told him to get out. I told him I hated him. No matter what I said, your father stuck with me. He is hardheaded! He made me look at my life and at myself. I was angry, but now I am thankful.

Wednesday, March 12

This afternoon, I looked through the want ads. After you are born, I want to work again. We need the money. When I go back to work, you will stay with your grandmother during the day. She is a loving, responsible woman. She can't wait to meet her first grandchild.

David, I'm starting to feel tired and clumsy. I think I'm getting bigger every day. The next few months will be hard, but I know you will be worth it. I can't wait to hold you in my arms.

▶ **Final Check-in**

Did Tina tell about the things you predicted in "Before You Read" on page 44? Did anything surprise you about her journal?

After You Read

A. Did the Journal Make Sense? Reread sections you marked with a question mark (?). Do they make sense now? If not, discuss them with a partner or your instructor.

B. Build Your Vocabulary Look at the words you underlined. Can you figure them out now? If not, find out what they are. Add them to your word bank.

C. Answer These Questions

1. Do you believe Tina will be a caring mother? _____

   Give one detail from Tina's journal that explains why you think the way you do.

   _____

2. Write an example from Tina's journal of
   a. information about Tina's past

   _____

   b. Tina's hopes and feelings for the future

   _____

3. Choose the statement Tina would likely agree with.
   (1) "Face up to your problems, and then move on."
   (2) "Don't trust people to stand by you."
   (3) "You can't change the way you are."

▶ **Talk About It**
Discuss the question below with a partner or small group.
If you like, write a response.

"Children are the future of the world." What does this statement mean to you?

Think About It: Draw Conclusions

You can draw a **conclusion** when you use information to decide something that you have not been told directly. For example, picture this:

- A man, a woman, and a child are walking together.
- The man and woman are holding the child's hands.
- The man and woman are wearing wedding rings.

What conclusion would you draw about how these people are related?

_____

It is reasonable to conclude that these three people are a family. The information about them walking together, holding hands, and wearing wedding rings supports this conclusion.

What conclusion can you draw from the information below?

- Your 15-year-old son keeps his bedroom door shut all the time.
- You find items used by people who abuse drugs in your son's backpack.
- You ask your son about the things you found, and he does not deny owning them.

Conclusion: _____

It is reasonable to conclude that your son has a drug problem.

Practice Read each paragraph below. Then check whether you can draw each conclusion based on the information given. If you think you can, write why.

A. ▶ My name is Tina. I am writing this journal as a gift for you, my baby boy. In four months, you will come into this world. Your father and I will name you David. In Hebrew, this name means "beloved one." I will write down my thoughts and experiences during the first years of your life.

1. Tina had a test to discover what sex her baby is.

   Is this a reasonable conclusion? _____ No _____ Yes, because

   _____

2. Tina is a very young woman.

   Is this a reasonable conclusion? _____ No _____ Yes, because

   _____

   B. ▶ I started drinking as a young teen. Your father never knew I had a problem until we moved in together. Then he suspected right away. When he confronted me, I lied. I told him to get out. I told him I hated him. No matter what I said, your father stuck with me. He is hardheaded! He made me look at my life and at myself.

3. Tina drank secretly when she first started going with David's father.

   Is this a reasonable conclusion? _____ No _____ Yes, because

   _____

4. Tina's husband is a strong, caring person.

   Is this a reasonable conclusion? _____ No _____ Yes, because

   _____

   C. ▶ This afternoon, I looked through the want ads. After you are born, I want to work again. We need the money. When I go back to work, you will stay with your grandmother during the day. She is a loving, responsible woman. She can't wait to meet her first grandchild.

5. Tina had worked before she became pregnant.

   Is this a reasonable conclusion? _____ No _____ Yes, because

   _____

6. David's grandmother is Tina's mother.

   Is this a reasonable conclusion? _____ No _____ Yes, because

   _____

Write About It: Write a Journal Entry

Like Tina, many people keep journals to write about their thoughts and feelings. Suppose you kept a journal. Write an entry in your journal for today.

A. Prewrite Think about what you want to write about. You could write about your children or your plans to have a child. You could write about your parents or grandparents. Jot down your topic here.

_____

B. Write Write your thoughts and feelings about your topic.

Today's Date: _____

_____

_____

_____

_____

_____

_____

_____

_____

_____

If you like, start to keep a personal journal.

▶ **Hold on to this work.** You may decide that you want to share it with others.

Word Work: Prefixes and Roots

Many longer words are made up of word parts called prefixes, roots, and suffixes. The **root** is the part that gives the basic meaning to the word. A **prefix** is a part added to the beginning of the root to give it a different meaning.

Prefix	Meaning	Example	New Meaning
anti-	against	antiwar	against war
mis-	wrongly, badly	misbehave	behave badly
pre-	before	prewriting	before writing
trans-	across	transport	carry across

Tip

When you come to a word you don't recognize, look for a prefix and a root. Read the root first. Then add the prefix to read the whole word. If you add the meaning of the prefix to the meaning of the root, you can usually figure out what the new word means.

Practice

A. Draw a line between the prefix and the root in each word below. Read the words aloud. Try to figure out the meanings of any unknown words.

1. predict
2. antifreeze
3. mistake
4. transform
5. prefix
6. antislavery
7. preview
8. translate
9. mischief
10. antibiotic
11. mislead
12. transpire

B. On separate paper, make as many words as you can from the prefixes and roots listed below. Use a dictionary if you wish.

Prefixes		Roots	
de-	re-	act	mit
in-	sub-	duce	scribe
per-	trans-	form	spect

Lesson 6

LEARNING GOALS

Strategy: Understand how another person feels
Reading: Read a story
Skill: Understand character
Writing: Describe a character
Word Work: Prefixes, roots, and suffixes

Before You Read

"Suspect" is a story about a father and son. The father is a police chief. Before you read "Suspect," think about the relationship between fathers and sons.

Name one thing that a father and son can do to develop a good relationship.

_____

Suppose a son does something to break the law. Describe two or three ways his father might feel.

_____

_____

Key Words Read each sentence. Do you know the underlined words?
- The <u>police officer</u> arrested the man for robbery.
- Could you explain the <u>situation</u> that was happening in the police station?
- A man was brought in for <u>questioning</u> about the crime.

Suspect

Jack Tanner sat in his office on a hot summer night. Jack was chief of police in Hillwood. He came from several generations of police officers. Jack's father had been police chief before him. Jack hoped that one or more of his three sons would join the force someday.

Jack was a good police chief. He was fair. He made decisions quickly and stuck with them. Jack was a confident leader. People trusted him.

Jack was 45 years old, but he looked older. Deep wrinkles covered his face. His hair was half gray. Tonight Jack was tired. As he stood up to leave, there was a knock on his open office door. He looked up to see Officer Wade, a young rookie.

"What is it, Wade?" Wade looked nervous and unsure.

Check-in ▶ How is Jack feeling now? Do you have a positive feeling about Jack?

"Sir, Officer Martin just brought in a robbery suspect. I think you should know that—." It was too late. Jack saw why Wade was nervous. The suspect was Jack's oldest son, Brian.

The police station was quiet. Jack walked toward his son. Brian was in handcuffs. An officer stood next to him.

Jack spoke firmly. "Officer Martin, could you please tell me the situation here?"

"Yes, sir. We got a call about a robbery at a gas station. We found this suspect running from the scene. We've brought him in for questioning."

Jack looked at Brian, then back at Officer Martin. "I think you know that this is my son. Before you begin questioning, I'd like to speak with him."

◀ **Check-in**

How do you think Jack is feeling now? What will he say to Brian?

Jack led Officer Martin and Brian into his office. He could not believe what was happening. He felt numb. Jack sat down at his desk. He waited for Brian to explain. Finally, he asked, "Brian, did you do this?" Brian said nothing. He did not even look at his father.

Jack became angry, but he stayed calm. He put his hand on his son's shoulder. "Brian, you have to talk to the officers. You need to tell them the truth. I'll be here when you're done. I'll put up your bail. We'll go home and talk about this."

When Brian had left, Jack fell back into his chair. If Brian was guilty, Jack would help him. Jack had helped dozens of men and women get their life back on track after a mistake. Jack made a promise to himself. No matter what happened, he would stand by his son.

▶ **Final Check-in**

How did Jack feel by the end of the story? Look at the responses you wrote in "Before You Read" on page 52. Do you think Jack felt some of the ways you described?

After You Read

A. Did the Story Make Sense? Reread sections you marked with a question mark (?). Do they make sense now? If not, discuss them with a partner or your instructor.

B. Build Your Vocabulary Look at the words you <u>underlined</u>. Can you figure them out now? If not, find out what they are. Add them to your word bank.

C. Answer These Questions

1. Match Jack's feelings with the situation.

Jack felt . . .	when . . .
a. concerned	_____ Brian did not talk or look at him.
b. numb	_____ he saw Officer Wade was nervous.
c. angry	_____ he realized Brian had been arrested.

2. Why might it be harder for Jack to have a son in trouble than it might be for another parent?

   (1) People expect a policeman's son to obey the law.

   (2) People trust Jack to be a strong leader.

   (3) Jack knows the law.

3. Which parent has a problem similar to Jack's?

   (1) a salesman whose son does not become a salesman

   (2) a teacher whose daughter is accused of cheating

   (3) a pilot whose son flies dangerous test flights

 Talk About It

In your own words, tell the story of Jack and his son to a classmate or friend. Then discuss whether you think Jack handled the situation with his son well.

Think About It: Understand Character

A **character** is a person in a story. In "Suspect," the main character is Jack. Writers create characters and describe them to you. Some of the kinds of information writers use to describe characters are given below. Check the ones that helped you learn about Jack.

_____ looks   _____ way of speaking

_____ job   _____ way of acting

_____ home life   _____ how he treats others

_____ interests   _____ how others feel about him

In the story, you learn these things about Jack:

Looks: He was 45 years old, but looked older. Deep wrinkles covered his face. His hair was half gray.

Job and home life: Jack was chief of police. He came from several generations of police officers. He hoped that one of his three sons would join the force someday.

Ways of acting and treating others: Jack was good and fair. He made decisions quickly and stuck with them. He was a confident leader. He had helped people get their lives back on track.

How others feel about him: People trusted him.

From this character description, you get to know Jack. What kind of man would you infer that Jack Tanner is?
(1) a decent man who thinks family is important
(2) a vain man who likes being chief more than anything

You probably answered (1). Jack is described as "good" and "fair," so he is a decent man. He followed in his family's line of work, and he hopes one of his sons will join him. So family is probably important to him.

Practice Read each character description. Then mark the statement **True** or **False.**

A. Brian Tanner, the chief's son, sat in the back of the squad car. The officers on duty were surprised to see him there. Brian was a good student. He was a star on the high school track team. He had never caused any trouble.

Did Brian rob the gas station? The officers didn't know. But they did know that Brian looked angry and confused tonight.

True   False

_____ _____ **1.** If Brian did rob the gas station, this action was "out of character," something you would not expect him to do.

_____ _____ **2.** Brian was a bright, hard-working young man.

B. Lou and Mike sat in the basement of Lou's house. They wondered what was happening to Brian.

"I can't believe they caught him," Lou said. "Maybe we shouldn't have left him outside the gas station."

"Are you kidding?" Mike said. "Brian is the chief's kid. They won't book him. Besides, we don't owe him anything."

"You're right," Lou said. He turned the stereo up and grabbed his drink. They listened to the music and forgot about Brian.

True   False

_____ _____ **3.** Brian's friends are concerned and caring people.

_____ _____ **4.** Lou and Mike stand by their friends.

Write About It: Describe a Character

You have read about Jack Tanner and his son Brian. Now create a character description of Jack's wife.

A. Prewrite Choose one set of descriptions for Susan Tanner. Add one or two details of your own.

Susan Tanner 1
- is a good-natured woman of 45
- spends much of her time at home with her children
- when told that Brian had been arrested, said, "I can't believe it. I want to talk with him right away."

_____

_____

_____

Susan Tanner 2
- is a woman whose social life means the most to her
- spends much of her time shopping and visiting with friends
- when told that Brian had been arrested, said, "I'm not surprised. I thought he had fallen in with the wrong crowd."

_____

_____

B. Write Copy your character description on your own paper. Add some sentences of your own that tell more about Susan Tanner.

▶ **Hold on to this work.** You may use it again at this end of this unit.

▶ **Talk About It**
Discuss the questions below with a partner or small group. If you like, write a response.

What do you think happened to Brian? Do you think either or both of his parents helped or supported him? Why or why not?

Word Work: Prefixes, Roots, and Suffixes

You studied prefixes and roots in Lesson 5. A **suffix** is a word part that is added to the end of a root. Suffixes change the meaning of the word.

brother + hood = brotherhood   wonder + ful = wonderful

Suffixes can also change how the word is spelled and used in a sentence.

I can't *decide* what job to do first. It is a hard *decision* to make.

Tip   When you don't recognize a word, look for a prefix, a root, and a suffix. Read the root first. Then add the prefix and the suffix. If you add the meanings of the prefix and the suffix to the meaning of the root, you can usually figure out what the word means.

Suffix	Meaning of Suffix	Example
-able	able to, capable of	affordable
-ion	act, result, or state of	inspection
-or	one who, person who	inspector
-ous	full of, characterized by	dangerous

Practice

A. Draw lines between the prefix, root, and suffix of each word below. Read the words aloud. Try to figure out the meanings of unfamiliar words.

   1. inventor   **3.** discussion   **5.** advantageous   **7.** reaction

   2. outrageous   **4.** dependable   **6.** contractor   **8.** transportable

B. On separate paper, make as many words as you can from the prefixes, roots, and suffixes listed below. Use a dictionary if you wish.

Prefixes	Roots	Suffixes
ex-	port	-able
in-	press	-ion
re-	spect	

▶ Writing Skills Mini-Lesson: Complex Sentences

A complex sentence has two parts: an independent clause and a dependent clause. A **clause** is a group of words containing a subject and a verb. You can write a **complex sentence** using a time word like *when:*

My parents were very young when they met.

1. **An independent clause is a complete thought. An independent clause could stand alone as a separate sentence.**

   Independent Clause: My parents were very young.

2. **A dependent clause is an incomplete thought. It can start with a time word like *when, while, before,* or *after.* A dependent clause is not a complete thought, so it cannot stand alone.**

   Dependent Clause: when they met

3. **Be sure to include a subject and a verb in each clause.**

   S V   S V
   My **parents were** very young when **they met.**

Practice On your own paper, copy and complete each complex sentence about your parents. Begin each sentence with "My mother" or "My father" or "My parents."

1. _____ while I was at school.

2. _____ when she was young.

3. _____ before I was born.

4. _____ after I was born.

5. _____ when I was a baby.

6. _____ when he was growing up.

7. _____ while I was growing up.

8. _____ after they got older.

Reading Review

This story is about something that people in every generation face.
Read it and answer the questions.

Nothing New

Gary and Trish had been married for seven years. They had
seen some good times together. But the last few years, they
always seemed to be fighting. Trish thought Gary spent too
much money. Gary felt Trish nagged him all the time. He had
started to think of getting a divorce. He went to his parents'
home to talk about it.

"Come on in," his father greeted him. His father's smile
faded when he saw the look on Gary's face. He listened
quietly as Gary told what he was thinking.

"You know, Gary, you sound like me many years ago.
There was a time when your mother and I almost got a
divorce."

"What!" Gary exclaimed.

"Oh, yes," his father went on. "Most marriages go through
a time like you're having now. But in the end, your mother
and I wouldn't let it happen. I think we were watching you
play one night. You were just two years old at the time. We
both then decided we had to make our marriage work. And
I've been happy we did for thirty years."

Gary thought of his own young son. "You're right, Dad.
At the least, Trish and I have to try harder."

1. What is the theme of this story?

    (1) Divorce is bad for children.

    (2) Fathers and sons are like each other.

    (3) Marriages have always demanded hard work.

2. Gary and his father have the kind of relationship where they

    (1) talk openly

    (2) fight often

    (3) keep apart

3. Can you reasonably conclude that Gary cares about his son?

    _____ No

    _____ Yes, because _____

Writing Process

In Unit 2, you wrote two first drafts. Choose the piece that you would like to work with more. You will revise, edit, and make a final copy of this draft.

    _____ your poem about family members (page 43)

    _____ your character description of Susan Tanner (page 58)

Find the first draft you chose. Then turn to page 128 in this book. Follow steps 3, 4, and 5 in the Writing Process to create a final draft.

As you revise, check your draft for this specific point:

Poem: Do your words create a clear picture of some members of your family?

Character description: Do the details you added tell more about Susan Tanner?

Unit 3 Voices for Justice

Someone who speaks out for what is right is a voice for justice. That person tries to see that justice is done and that everyone is treated fairly. In this unit, you will read about several people who have raised their voices for justice.

People who are voices for justice may become famous. Martin Luther King, Jr., and Cesar Chavez are two well-known examples. Other people have spoken out for justice, but they are not famous. Yet their work is important, too.

People who speak out for justice make the world a fairer place to live. Think about your own life. Have you met any people who have raised their voices for justice? Have you ever raised your own voice for what you believe is right?

▶ **Be an Active Reader**
As you read the selections in this unit
- Put a question mark (?) by things you do not understand.
- Underline words you do not know. Try to use context clues to figure them out.

Lesson 7

LEARNING GOALS

Strategy: Predict what you might read about
Reading: Read a story
Skill: Identify setting
Writing: Describe a setting
Word Work: Dividing words into syllables

Before You Read

In the story "A Safe Place," a woman named Clara Ramos is working for justice. She has started a women's shelter. It is a place where women can feel safe from violent husbands or boyfriends.

Before you read this story, think about violence in the home. With a partner or small group, discuss what you know about it. Is it common? What are some causes? How can families get help?

What do you think will be in a story about a women's shelter? Check each thing you might read about.

_____ characters who need shelter from violent partners

_____ information on how to start a shelter

_____ a description of a shelter

_____ a problem between a husband and wife

_____ facts about the rate of violence in the home

Key Words Read each sentence. Do you know the underlined words?

- Women sat relaxing in the large <u>comfortable</u> front room of the house.
- Some children watched TV while <u>several</u> women talked.
- In some homes, <u>domestic</u> <u>violence</u> occurs.

A Safe Place

Clara Ramos heard a knock on the door. When she opened it, a woman was on the front step. The woman was looking over her shoulder, as if someone were following her. When she turned to face the door, Clara could see she was young and frightened.

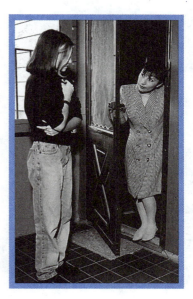

"Welcome to Clara's House," Clara said in a strong but gentle voice. "I'm Clara. What's your name?" In a quiet voice, the young woman answered, "Jane."

Clara led Jane inside. The large front room of the house was comfortable and sunny. Several women relaxed on sofas, chatting. Some children sat on the floor, watching TV. A few of the women smiled at Jane.

"Jane," Clara said, "are you here to get away from someone who is hurting you?"

Jane brushed aside her brown hair and nodded yes. Clara could see her eye had been bruised. Suddenly Jane walked over to the front window and looked out. Then she gasped and stepped back. "I knew it!" Jane cried. "Mick is here. He followed me. I don't know what to do."

Clara said, "Jane, if you like, I'll see to it that Mick leaves. You do not have to see him."

"Yes, yes," Jane said. "Please make him go. He hasn't been drinking, so he'll probably leave."

What do you think will happen next? Will Mick leave? Will something happen to Jane or Clara?

◀ **Check-in**

When Clara returned, she said, "Jane, Mick agreed to leave for now, but he will probably come back. You must decide what you want. I'm here to help you do that."

Jane thought. Then she said, "I used to think I was lucky to have Mick. When he started beating me, I told myself his anger was my fault. Now I'm not so sure."

"Mick's anger is his own problem," Clara said. "It's not your fault. No one has the right to hurt you. You have the right to help yourself, to make choices. For one thing, you can choose to stay here. You can stay for one night—or a year."

That evening, Jane was in the front room of Clara's House. A woman approached her and said she had a phone call. It was Mick. "Baby, please come home," Jane heard Mick plead. "I won't drink anymore. I promise I won't hit you anymore."

His voice sounded so sweet to Jane.

What will Jane do? Do you think she will stay in Clara's House or go back to Mick?

◀ **Check-in**

Then Jane looked around. Posters hung on the walls of the house. They had messages, such as "Domestic Violence Is a Crime" and "You Control Your Own Life." Jane remembered the other times Mick had said, "Oh, baby, I promise." She also remembered Clara's words from that morning. "No one has the right to hurt you. You have the right to help yourself."

Jane made a decision. She would stay in Clara's House, at least for a while. She needed time to think. If Mick changed in that time, then good for him. For now, Jane cared only about changing her own life.

▶ **Final Check-in**

Look at the items you checked in "Before You Read" on page 64. Which of them were in the story? Did the other predictions you made as you were reading come true?

After You Read

A. Did the Story Make Sense? Reread sections you marked with a question mark (?). Do they make sense now? If not, discuss them with a partner or your instructor.

B. Build Your Vocabulary Look at the words you underlined. Can you figure them out now? If not, find out what they are. Add them to your word bank.

C. Answer These Questions

1. Did you predict Jane would stay at Clara's House? _____ Write one thing from the story that helped you make your prediction.

_____

_____

2. Clara Ramos is a voice for justice because she
   (1) greets Jane at the door of the shelter
   (2) talks to Jane about her rights
   (3) tells Mick to come back later

3. Choose the four most important events in the story from the items below. Write them on a sheet of paper. Use your list to help you tell the story to a partner.

Jane comes to Clara's House.   Mick calls Jane.
Some women smile at Jane.   Posters hang on the wall.
Clara tells Jane she can choose   Jane decides to stay.
to stay.

▶ **Talk About It**
Discuss the questions below with a partner or small group.
If you like, write a response.

Jane wonders if she should leave Mick. Is Jane's choice hard?
Why or why not? What advice would you give Jane?

Think About It: Identify Setting

In a story, the time and place make up the **setting.** For example, the setting of "A Safe Place" is one day in a women's shelter.

Think about this setting. Use ideas from the story and your imagination to complete these sentences.

The front room of Clara's House is _____

_____

_____

It has posters on the walls that _____

_____

The story tells you that the front room is large, comfortable, and sunny. It says the posters have messages about family violence and controlling your own life. You could add that there are sofas. Perhaps you imagined other details that weren't stated in the story.

The setting of a story can make you feel a certain way. For example, the front room of Clara's House seems pleasant, warm, and safe. This safe feeling helped Jane decide to stay.

To see how different settings can make you feel, imagine you are in each of these settings:
- a dark, smoky nightclub
- a candlelit dinner for two in a small restaurant
- a department store during a huge sale
- a ball park during the World Series
- a courtroom just before a jury gives its decision

Discuss your feelings with a partner or small group.

Practice Read each short paragraph. Then answer the questions about the setting.

A. Jane sat in the front room at Clara's House. Two little girls played on the floor. Jane was writing a list of her job skills. She hoped to find a job soon. On her paper, Jane wrote "fast typist," "good with numbers," and "dependable." She looked up to think a bit. The bright, cozy room made her think of how her life had changed. Then, at the bottom of the list, Jane wrote "survivor."

1. What is the setting? _____

_____

2. This setting feels
   (1) strained
   (2) pleasant
   (3) dark

B. It was late on a Saturday night. The doors to the emergency room flew open. A gunshot victim was rushed in on a stretcher. He had been shot by his wife. The doctor tore open the victim's shirt. Her face was grim. She began to work quickly. Everyone in the room was quiet. They knew the man might not live.

3. What is the setting? _____

_____

4. This setting feels
   (1) tense
   (2) joyful
   (3) peaceful

5. Write three details that support your choice for number 4. _____

_____

Write About It: Describe a Setting

You have read about the setting of Clara's House. Now write about
a setting of your own.

A. Prewrite Think about a place where you spend a lot of your time
each day. Fill in details on the lines below.

What the place is _____

What you do in the place _____

What the place looks like _____

_____

Objects in the place _____

_____

The feeling the place gives you _____

_____

B. Write Use your answers above to complete the following paragraph
on your own paper. Add more details to describe the setting if you like.

I spend a lot of my time _____ because I

_____ there. It looks _____. Some

things in it are _____. This place gives me a

feeling of _____ because _____.

Give your description to someone to read. Ask this person to describe
the setting back to you. Did he or she get a good picture of the place?
Why or why not?

▶ **Hold on to this work.** You may use it again at the end of this unit.

Word Work: Dividing Words into Syllables

A **syllable** is a word part that has one vowel sound. You can divide words with two or more syllables into those smaller parts. Here are some tips:

Tip 1 Each syllable has only one vowel sound. Divide between vowels that have separate sounds. Read these words aloud.

      qui et   i de a   re al i ty   co op er ate

Tip 2 Do not divide between vowel pairs that make one sound:

A. Common long vowel pairs: *ai, ee, ea, oa,* and *oo*

      main tain   free dom   eas i er   car toon

B. Other common vowel pairs: *au, oi, oy,* and *ou*

      au thor   poi son   boy cott   coun cil

Tip 3 Do not divide vowel-consonant clusters: *ar, er, ir, or, ur, aw, ow, al*

      par ent   A mer i can   tow el   al so

Practice Read these words aloud. Write the number of syllables you hear in front of each word. Draw lines where you divide the syllables.

_____ 1. weary	_____ 9. thousand	_____ 17. drowsy
_____ 2. avoid	_____ 10. partner	_____ 18. lawyer
_____ 3. greedy	_____ 11. furnish	_____ 19. ceremony
_____ 4. throat	_____ 12. restraint	_____ 20. audience
_____ 5. radio	_____ 13. violence	_____ 21. maintenance
_____ 6. reason	_____ 14. mountain	_____ 22. although
_____ 7. shampoo	_____ 15. cocoon	_____ 23. coordinate
_____ 8. between	_____ 16. cousin	_____ 24. experience

Lesson 8

LEARNING GOALS

Strategy: Use what you know to understand what you read
Reading: Read a biography
Skill: Understand the main idea and details
Writing: Write an interview
Word Work: More dividing words into syllables

Before You Read

"Voice of a People" is a biography of South African leader Nelson Mandela. You know that a biography is a piece of writing about a person's life. The prefix *bio-* means *life*. The root *graph* means *writing*.

Before you read Nelson Mandela's biography, think of what you already know about him and his country, South Africa. Check each fact you know something about.

_____ South Africa had a system called apartheid [uh PART hayt].

_____ Under apartheid, people of different races had separate housing, schools, jobs, and public transit.

_____ Blacks and other nonwhites had almost no rights.

_____ Blacks were kept very poor.

Add something else you know about South Africa. Add what you know about Nelson Mandela, too.

_____

_____

Key Words Read each sentence. Do you know the underlined words?
- The people began to <u>boycott</u> goods in protest.
- Damaging a railroad is an act of <u>sabotage</u>.
- After Mandela was arrested, he was <u>imprisoned</u>.

▶ **Use the Strategy**

To help you understand the biography of Nelson Mandela, think of what you already know about him and his country. See if it helps you understand new information.

Voice of a People

NELSON MANDELA

For many years, people of different races lived apart in South Africa. In 1948, whites made this system of apartheid the law. Blacks could not even go into white neighborhoods without passes.

Thousands of people fought to end this unjust system. Thousands also died. Nelson Mandela led the fight against apartheid. Mandela's amazing life inspired millions of people.

Check-in ▶ What do you already know about apartheid? Why would people fight and even die to end it?

A Young Leader

Nelson Mandela was born in 1918 in South Africa. His father was a tribal chief. Mandela grew up to become a lawyer. When he was 26 years old, he joined a group called the African National Congress (ANC). The ANC wanted justice for blacks. Mandela began to lead nonviolent protests to fight for justice. He called for peaceful strikes, boycotts, and marches.

Mandela's work made him famous among blacks. His name also became known to the white South African government. The police began to watch him closely. During those years, Mandela and other ANC members were often arrested and beaten.

In 1960, 69 blacks were killed by police during a protest in an area called Sharpeville. Mandela and the ANC then decided that nonviolent action was not enough. They turned to sabotage to make the government change. They began to damage public works, such as railroads and power plants. But they tried to avoid harming innocent people.

A Famous Prisoner

In 1962, the police arrested Mandela. Two years later, he was sentenced to life in prison. Mandela was 45 years old.

Mandela was imprisoned at a labor camp called Robben Island. For 10 years, he swung a pickax in a limestone quarry. But he also tried to work for change inside the prison. He tried to gain better conditions for inmates. He continued to inspire the blacks of South Africa.

In the 1970s and 1980s, people around the world began to speak out against apartheid. Many began to boycott South African goods. By the mid-1980s, many countries stopped doing business with South Africa. The world wanted the country to change. Finally, a new president of South Africa, F. W. De Klerk, was elected. De Klerk realized that apartheid must end.

Think about what you know about Nelson Mandela, about political groups that do acts of sabotage, about boycotts, and about South Africa. Is your knowledge helping you understand this biography better?

◀ Check-in

In February 1990, President De Klerk released Nelson Mandela. After more than 27 years of being imprisoned, Mandela was free. He and De Klerk began working on a plan to change the government and bring more power to blacks. Soon after, apartheid also came to an end. After years of struggle and violence, a new South Africa could begin.

President of a Nation

SOUTH AFRICANS IN LINE
WAITING TO VOTE

A SOUTH AFRICAN
WOMAN VOTING

In May 1994, an important event happened. For the first time, South Africans of all races could vote for president. People worried that violence would break out on election day. But the voting was peaceful. And the people of South Africa elected Nelson Mandela president.

At the time, millions of blacks lived in small shacks. Most did not have running water or electric power in their homes. The average wage was less than $220 a month. As South Africa's new president, Mandela promised to work for all races. "Our message," he said, "is that the basic needs of the . . . people" must be met.

Nelson Mandela's amazing life will not be forgotten. The former prisoner who became the leader of a nation risked his life by raising his voice for justice.

▶ **Final Check-in**
Did your knowledge of Nelson Mandela and South Africa help you understand his biography? What new information about Mandela did you learn?

After You Read

A. Did the Biography Make Sense? Reread sections you marked with a question mark (?). Do they make sense now? If not, discuss them with a partner or your instructor.

B. Build Your Vocabulary Look at the words you <u>underlined</u>. Can you figure them out now? If not, find out what they are. Add them to your word bank.

C. Answer These Questions

1. The biography says, "Thousands of people fought to end this unjust system." Use what you know about apartheid to explain why it was unjust.

_____

_____

2. Which term best describes Mandela's life?
   (1) disappointing
   (2) inspiring
   (3) carefree

3. Which of the following facts helps explain why Mandela's life could be called "amazing"?
   (1) He went from rebel to prisoner to president.
   (2) He spent 27 years in prison.
   (3) He fought apartheid with acts of sabotage.

▶ **Talk About It**

Discuss the statement below with a partner or small group. If you like, write a response.

"A child that is just born cannot be expected to run."—a saying among black South Africans after Nelson Mandela's government began its work.

Think About It: Understand the Main Idea and Details

In Lesson 3, you learned that a paragraph has a **main idea** that is the most important point, and supporting **details** that explain, or support, the main idea. Longer readings often follow a similar overall plan. They have a **title** and often are divided into parts that have **headings.** We can think of the title as expressing the main idea. The headings indicate major details that support the main idea of the whole reading. You can picture "Voice of a People" like this:

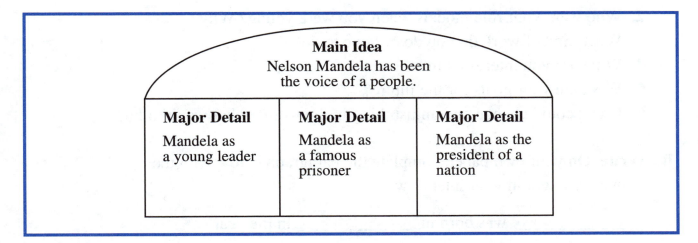

Main Idea
Nelson Mandela has been the voice of a people.

Major Detail	**Major Detail**	**Major Detail**
Mandela as a young leader	Mandela as a famous prisoner	Mandela as the president of a nation

Practice Each of these major details has supporting details of its own. Listed below are several supporting details from the reading. Write each one under the heading that it supports.

- sentenced to life in prison at 45
- led nonviolent protests for justice
- promised to work for all races
- began to sabotage
- was elected president in 1994
- worked to improve inmate conditions

A Young Leader

_____   _____

A Famous Prisoner

_____   _____

President of a Nation

_____   _____

Write About It: Write an Interview

How does someone write a biography? They read about the person they are writing about. If they can, they talk to that person. They ask questions. Below are some questions that biographers might ask when they interview someone. Use them to write an interview.

A. Prewrite Interview a friend or classmate by asking these questions. Take notes on the answers.

1. When and where were you born?
2. Who were your role models when you were young? Why?
3. What kind of work do you do or hope to do?
4. What are you interested in?
5. What are your goals for the future?
6. If you could change one unjust thing in the world, what would it be?

B. Write On your own paper, complete the paragraph below with the answers you got in your interview.

_____ was born in _____ in the year _____. When _____ was young, his/her most important role model was _____ because _____.

Today he/she _____ and is interested in _____.

In the future, _____ hopes to _____.

If _____ could change one thing about the world, it would be _____.

▶ **Hold on to this work.** You may use it again at this end of this unit.

Word Work: More Dividing Words into Syllables

Here are some more tips on how to divide unfamiliar words into syllables:

Tip 1 Divide between double consonants.

dol lar   ham mer   mes sage   mir ror

Tip 2 When three consonants come together, divide between a single consonant and a consonant blend or digraph.

coun try   chil dren   mer chant   judg ment

Tip 3 Divide *before* a consonant followed by *le* at the end of a word.

dou ble   gen tle   jun gle   peo ple

Notice: the last syllable of these words is pronounced like *ul:* [bul], [tul], [gul], [pul].

Practice Read these words aloud. Write the number of syllables you hear in front of each word. Draw lines where you divide the syllables.

_____ **1.** marble	_____ **13.** middle	_____ **25.** sprinkle
_____ **2.** surprise	_____ **14.** athletic	_____ **26.** setting
_____ **3.** bubble	_____ **15.** hundred	_____ **27.** unstable
_____ **4.** knowledge	_____ **16.** address	_____ **28.** supplier
_____ **5.** alphabet	_____ **17.** candle	_____ **29.** laughter
_____ **6.** sudden	_____ **18.** pantry	_____ **30.** possible
_____ **7.** district	_____ **19.** better	_____ **31.** griddle
_____ **8.** coffee	_____ **20.** pumpkin	_____ **32.** transformation
_____ **9.** huddle	_____ **21.** department	_____ **33.** difference
_____ **10.** friendlier	_____ **22.** prettier	_____ **34.** wrinkle
_____ **11.** hardly	_____ **23.** trouble	_____ **35.** merchandise
_____ **12.** winner	_____ **24.** flammable	_____ **36.** disappear

Lesson 9

LEARNING GOALS

Strategy: Understand how a speaker feels
Reading: Read two speeches
Skill: Identify viewpoint
Writing: Write your viewpoint

Before You Read

In the 1800s, the United States fought with Native Americans. The U.S. took their land and forced them to live on reservations. These pieces of land were often hundreds of miles from their homeland.

The first reading in this lesson is a speech made by Chief Joseph during this time. Chief Joseph belonged to the Nez Perce [NEZ PERS] tribe of the Northwest. He tried to lead his people to Canada to escape being sent to a reservation. But the army stopped them 20 miles from the border. The Nez Perce were sent to a faraway reservation. Many of them died there.

Before you read Chief Joseph's speech, think of what you know about the experience of Native Americans. Then read each statement below. Check whether you agree or disagree with it.

Agree **Disagree**

_____ _____ The U.S. government treated Native Americans unfairly in the 1800s.

_____ _____ Native Americans should be given back some of the land that was taken from them.

Key Word Read this sentence. Do you know the underlined word?
  • The people wanted to follow their own <u>religion</u>.

Use the Strategy

In this speech, a Native American leader speaks out about justice. To help you understand his view, put yourself in his shoes. Try to feel as he felt.

Let Me Be a Free Man

Chief Joseph

[Government officials] all say they are my friends, and that I shall have justice, but while their mouths all talk right I do not understand why nothing is done for my people. . . .

CHIEF JOSEPH

Good words do not last long unless they amount to something. Words do not pay for my dead people. They do not pay for my country, now overrun by white men. . . . Good words will not give my people good health and stop them from dying. Good words will not get my people a home where they can live in peace and take care of themselves. . . . I have asked some of the great white chiefs where they get their authority to say to the Indian that he shall stay in one place, while he sees white men going where they please. They cannot tell me.

Let me be a free man—free to travel, free to stop, free to work, free to trade where I choose, free to choose my own teachers, free to follow the religion of my fathers, free to think and talk and act for myself.

 Check-in

If you were Chief Joseph, how would you feel about what had happened to your people? How would you feel toward white people? Go back to the statements you agreed or disagreed with on page 80. Have you changed your mind?

After You Read

A. Did the Speech Make Sense? Reread sections you marked with a question mark (?). Do they make sense now? If not, discuss them with a partner or your instructor.

B. Build Your Vocabulary Look at the words you <u>underlined</u>. Can you figure them out now? If not, find out what they are. Add them to your word bank.

C. Answer These Questions

1. Which of the following phrases best describes how Chief Joseph feels in this speech?
   (1) scared and worried
   (2) sad and beaten down
   (3) proud and defiant

2. Chief Joseph does not understand how white people can make Native Americans
   (1) work
   (2) live in peace
   (3) stay on reservations

3. Native American children were made to go to special schools and learn English. Which words from the speech tell you that Chief Joseph thought this was unjust?

_____

 Talk About It

Discuss the questions below with a partner or small group.
If you like, write a response.

"Good words do not last long unless they amount to something."
What does Chief Joseph mean by this? Does everyone have the
right to the freedoms Chief Joseph lists in the last paragraph?
Why or why not?

Think About It: Identify Viewpoint

Do we live in a just or an unjust society? Your answer to this question is based on your viewpoint. A **viewpoint** is a belief or an opinion about a topic.

Think about Chief Joseph's speech. What was his viewpoint about what white people say?

    (1) Their words are honest and true.

    (2) Their promises are worthless.

Chief Joseph says, ". . . while their mouths all talk right I do not understand why nothing is done for my people." So his viewpoint is that the promises of white people are worthless.

Now think again of your answer to the question at the top of this page. Why do you hold this view? You hold it because of:

- who you are
- what you have seen or heard or done
- what has happened to you
- what you have learned

You look at this society in a certain way because of your viewpoint. If you were someone else, you might have a different view of society.

You can understand Chief Joseph's viewpoint about white people by seeing them from his perspective:

- Who is Chief Joseph? He is a Native American leader.
- What has he seen happen to his people? They have been forced to live on a reservation. Many have died.
- What has he heard government officials tell him? They have told him they are his friends and that he will have justice.

Now answer this question yourself:

- What has been done for his people since Chief Joseph talked to the officials?

From his speech, you know that nothing has been done for his people. From that viewpoint, you can better understand why Chief Joseph views white people the way he does.

Practice Sitting Bull was the leader of the Sioux [SOO] Indians. Read the following speech for his views.

> When I was a boy, the Sioux owned the world; the sun rose and set on their land; they sent ten thousand men to battle. Where are the warriors today? Who slew them? Where are our lands? Who owns them? . . . Is it wrong for me to love my own? Is it wicked for me because my skin is red? Because I am a Sioux; because I was born where my father lived; because I would die for my people and my country?

> If the Great Spirit had desired me to be a white man he would have made me so in the first place. He put in your heart certain wishes and plans, in my heart he put other and different desires. Each man is good in his sight. It is not necessary for eagles to be crows.

Choose the best answer for each question.

1. In Sitting Bull's view, white people are
   (1) different from the Sioux
   (2) like eagles and crows
   (3) not good in the sight of the Great Spirit

2. Sitting Bull's viewpoint is shaped by the fact that he
   (1) desires to be a white man
   (2) belongs to the once-powerful Sioux
   (3) sent 10,000 men into battle

3. Sitting Bull's viewpoint is also shaped by the belief that
   (1) he should have been born a white man
   (2) people are intended to be different from each other
   (3) it is wrong for him to love his people

Write About It: Write Your Viewpoint

You have read the views of two Native American leaders. They were voices for justice. Now be a voice for justice yourself. Write a paragraph about your views on the need for justice.

A. Prewrite Choose a topic from the list below or one of your own.
- the treatment of Native Americans
- another group that is being treated unjustly
- a person you know or have heard about who is being treated unjustly

Answer these questions to get ideas to write about.

Who is the person or group that is being treated unjustly?

_____

Who treats this person or group unjustly?

_____

How is this person or group being treated unjustly?

_____

_____

What should be done to end the unjust treatment?

_____

_____

B. Write On your own paper, use your answers to write a paragraph about the need for justice.

▶ **Hold on to this work.** You may use it again at the end of this unit.

▶Writing Skills Mini-Lesson: More on Complex Sentences

As you learned in Unit 2, a **complex sentence** has both a dependent clause and an independent clause. The dependent clause can come first or last in the sentence.

1. **If you put the dependent clause first, use a comma between the clauses. Pause at the comma when you read aloud.**
   * **When the school closed,** the parents protested.

2. **If you put the dependent clause at the end of a sentence, don't use a comma.**
   * The parents protested **when the school closed.**

3. **Besides time words like *when,* you can use words like *because, although, if,* and *since* in the dependent clause.** These words show the relationship between the two thoughts in the sentence.
   * The students did well **because** the teachers cared.
   * **Although** the school was small, it had a fine library.
   * **If** parents get involved, they can make a difference.

Practice On your own paper, combine each pair of clauses below in two ways to make complex sentences. Put the dependent clause first in one sentence and last in the other. Use capital letters, commas, and periods correctly. The first one is done as an example.

Dependent Clause	Independent Clause
1. since the school was small	the students all knew each other

   <u>Since the school was small, the students all knew each other.</u>

   <u>The students all knew each other since the school was small.</u>

2. although some parents were silent	most parents spoke out
3. because the families protested	the school reopened
4. if a school closes	the children lose
5. because they enjoyed school	the children did well
6. although it needed repairs	the school was reopened
7. if they work together	parents can get things done
8. since the parents helped	the repairs were quickly made

Unit 3 Review

Reading Review

This reading is about a person who raised his voice for justice. Read it and then answer the questions.

Defending the Poor

Luis Galvan is a public defender, a lawyer for people in trouble with the law who cannot afford to pay. The government pays him with tax money instead. Luis's job requires him to be a good lawyer. He also acts as a social worker much of the time.

Luis is a skilled lawyer. He knows the law and works for his clients every step of the way. He is there from the first hearing through the trial. If his client is found guilty, Luis handles the appeal.

Because Luis has so much to do, he spends long hours at his work. He often spends all morning and part of the afternoon in court with clients. The rest of the day, he visits clients in jail and writes legal papers. But the legal work is not all that keeps Luis busy.

Luis also helps many of his clients get into drug programs, job-training programs, or get other help they need. Why does he do these extra things? Luis says, "The payoff comes when people call you years later and tell you how well they're doing."

We need more public defenders like Luis Galvan.

1. What is the main idea of this reading?

   (1) A public defender is paid with tax money.

   (2) Luis Galvan does his job of public defender well.

   (3) Luis Galvan is in court all morning.

2. Check the three details that support the main idea.

   _____ is a good lawyer   _____ works long hours   _____ is poor

   _____ gets tax money   _____ ignores his clients   _____ acts as a social worker

3. Mark this statement **True** or **False.**

   True   False

   _____   _____ The writer thinks public defenders are a waste of tax money.

Writing Process

In Unit 3, you wrote three first drafts. Choose the piece that you would like to work with more. You will revise, edit, and make a final copy of this draft.

   _____ your description of a familiar setting (page 70)

   _____ your biographical interview (page 78)

   _____ your paragraph about the need for justice (page 85)

Find the first draft you chose. Then turn to page 128 in this book. Follow steps 3, 4, and 5 in the Writing Process to create a final draft.

As you revise, check your draft for this specific point:

Setting description: Do your details give a clear picture of this place?

Interview: Did you include the important information from the interview?

Paragraph: Do you make clear how this person or group is being treated unjustly?

Unit 4 Express Yourself

When you see a movie or TV show you like, what do you do? You probably tell someone what you think about it. When you feel angry or happy or sad about something, what do you do? You may want to tell someone how you feel. In both cases, you express yourself.

Some people express themselves with words by speaking or writing about their thoughts and feelings. Some people express themselves through art or music. People even express themselves through the clothes they wear.

In Unit 4, different people express themselves by writing about their thoughts and feelings. You will read a reviewer's opinion of a TV show, a soldier's ideas about war, and a woman's feelings about being separated from someone she loves. Before you start the unit, think of your own thoughts and feelings. What moves you strongly enough to want to express yourself?

▶ **Be an Active Reader**
As you read the selections in this unit
- Put a question mark (?) by things you do not understand.
- <u>Underline</u> words you do not know. Try to use context clues to figure them out.

Lesson 10

LEARNING GOALS

Strategy: Use what you know to understand what you read
Reading: Read a review
Skill: Identify viewpoint
Writing: Write a review
Word Work: Review of dividing words into syllables

Before You Read

"Marian Anderson: A Tribute" is a review of a TV show. A tribute honors a person. Marian Anderson was an African American who became one of the world's leading concert singers.

"Marian Anderson: A Tribute" is a newspaper review. Do you ever read reviews of shows in a newspaper or a TV guide? Check each kind of information that a review of a TV show would probably give.

_____ what day the show is on

_____ what time the show is on

_____ what the show is about

_____ who stars in the show

_____ the reviewer's opinion of the show

_____ how much the show cost to make

Key Words Read each sentence. Do you know the underlined words?

- Anderson became a <u>symbol</u>, a person who stands for an idea.
- A <u>documentary</u> film about the life of Marian Anderson was on TV.
- Anderson had <u>dignity</u>, self-respect, and a <u>marvelous</u> voice.

▶ **Use the Strategy**

To understand this review better, notice what information it gives. Is it the same type of information you have seen in other reviews?

Marian Anderson: A Tribute

MARIAN ANDERSON

On Easter Sunday in 1939, Marian Anderson sang at the Lincoln Memorial in Washington, D.C. On that cold spring day, 75,000 people came outdoors to hear her. Anderson sang religious songs, such as "Gospel Train." She sang patriotic songs, such as "America." On that day, Anderson gave a wonderful concert. She also became a symbol of the civil rights movement in the U.S.

Tonight at 8:00 P.M., a TV documentary brings Anderson's story and her marvelous voice into our homes. "Marian Anderson: A Tribute" is in three parts. Each part covers a period in Anderson's life.

Check-in ▶ What information has the review just given you? What do you think the reviewer will talk about next?

Part 1 tells how Anderson grew up in Philadelphia. Her family was poor. There was no money for music lessons. Anderson once recalled, "I made up my own music. It was all in my head, but that was enough." Part 1 helps us see Anderson as a real person. We are touched by her strength and dignity.

Part 2 tells how Anderson began her career. Like many singers at that time, she studied and performed in Europe. There she won praise, awards, and thousands of fans. There was even "Marian Fever" in Sweden. I did not know this about Anderson, and I am a big fan of hers. Several recordings from this period display the power and beauty of her voice.

Part 3 is by far the longest. It tells how Anderson became a symbol for civil rights. Anderson had become a famous concert singer. But a group called the Daughters of the American Revolution (DAR) would not let her sing in their Washington, D.C., concert hall. What was their reason? She was African American. Eleanor Roosevelt, wife of President Franklin Roosevelt, stepped in to help. Mrs. Roosevelt used her power as First Lady. She set up a free outdoor concert for Anderson at the Lincoln Memorial.

The documentary may stress the Lincoln Memorial concert too much. There is little time left to complete Anderson's story. For instance, viewers do not learn that she was a U.S. delegate to the United Nations. And they do not hear that she won the U.N. Peace Prize in 1977.

Still "Marian Anderson: A Tribute" is an important documentary to watch. It is a powerful story about civil rights. It is a moving story about one woman's great talent and dignity. The music is marvelous. It is not to be missed.

▶ **Final Check-in**

Think about the information the review gave. Was it the information you checked in "Before You Read" on page 90? Was this review like other reviews you have read?

After You Read

A. Did the Review Make Sense? Reread sections you marked with a question mark (?). Do they make sense now? If not, discuss them with a partner or your instructor.

B. Build Your Vocabulary Look at the words you underlined. Can you figure them out now? If not, find out what they are. Add them to your word bank.

C. Answer These Questions

1. List two things you read in the review that you expected to read about.

_____

_____

Mark these statements **True** or **False**.

True   False

_____ _____ **2.** The documentary showed that Marian Anderson became a famous singer because of her family and background.

_____ _____ **3.** The reviewer would probably agree that this documentary is interesting mainly to singers and musicians.

 Talk About It

Discuss the question below with a partner or small group. If you like, write a response.

Based on the review, how did each of these people express herself?
- the reviewer
- Marian Anderson
- Eleanor Roosevelt

Think About It: Identify Viewpoint

As you learned in Lesson 9, a **viewpoint** is a belief or an opinion based on a person's life experiences. For example, when you watch a TV show, your viewpoint will determine whether or not you like the show.

The reviewer of "Marian Anderson: A Tribute" thought the show was good. Her review was positive. She had more good things to say about the show than bad:

Things the Reviewer Liked

- shows Anderson as a real person, with dignity
- tells reviewer something she did not already know
- important documentary
- powerful and moving story
- _____

Things the Reviewer Didn't Like

- spent too much time on concert
- did not complete Anderson's story

Find one more positive thing the reviewer said about the show in the last paragraph. Write it in the chart.

Did you write "the music is marvelous" in the chart?

The reviewer wrote from the viewpoint many reviewers use. She looked for both good and bad points. She wanted to let readers know if she thought they should watch the show.

The reviewer also wrote from the viewpoint of someone who likes Marian Anderson. Which line in the review helps you see that?

_____

_____

Did you see that "I am a big fan of hers" helps tell the reviewer's viewpoint?

Practice Read these reviews from a panel of people who watched "Marian Anderson: A Tribute." Then answer the questions about their opinions and viewpoints.

Michael Keller, 35, music teacher: "Anyone who loves music would have loved this show. I think the best moments were clips of Anderson singing. Hearing her voice is a wonderful experience."

Hector Diaz, 16, student: "The show was excellent. We're learning about the civil rights movement in school right now. This show gave me a close-up view of what happened to an important person. I was impressed."

Jody Jones, 24, computer programmer: "I didn't think the show was very good. I don't really like that kind of music. I guess the civil rights part was interesting, but not enough to make me enjoy watching the show."

1. a. Is Mr. Keller's view of the show mainly positive or negative? _____
  Underline two ideas in the review that explain your answer.

  b. Does anything about Mr. Keller help explain his viewpoint? _____

  If yes, what? _____

2. a. Is Mr. Diaz's view of the show mainly positive or negative? _____
  Underline two ideas in the review that explain your answer.

  b. Does anything about Mr. Diaz help explain his viewpoint? _____

  If yes, what? _____

3. a. Is Ms. Jones's view of the show mainly positive or negative? _____
  Underline two ideas in the review that explain your answer.

  b. Does anything about Ms. Jones help explain her viewpoint? _____

  If yes, what? _____

Write About It: Write a Review

The reviewer of "Marian Anderson: A Tribute" had both good and bad things to say about the show. Now write a review of something you have seen or read. It could be a TV show, a movie, or a reading from this book.

A. Prewrite Think about what you liked and what you did not like. Fill in this chart.

A Review of _____

by _____

Things I Liked

_____

_____

_____

_____

_____

_____

Things I Didn't Like

_____

_____

_____

_____

_____

_____

B. Write Use your chart to write a short review on your own paper.

▶ **Hold on to this work.** You may use it again at the end of this unit.

Word Work: Review of Dividing Words into Syllables

Here are tips you have learned for dividing unfamiliar words into syllables:

Tips

1. Divide between vowels that have separate sounds: i de a   qui et
2. Do not divide between vowel pairs that make one sound:
   a. Long vowel pairs: eas i er   mov ie
   b. Other vowel pairs: poi son   coun cil
3. Do not divide vowel-consonant clusters: par ent   tow el
4. Divide between double consonants: dol lar
5. Divide between a consonant and a blend or digraph: mer chant
6. Divide before a consonant plus *le* at the end of a word: cou ple

▶ **Remember:** There are exceptions to all these tips. If you say a word you don't recognize the first time you try, try another pronunciation. Keep trying until you hear a word you recognize. Then check it against the context of the reading or in a dictionary.

Practice Read these words aloud. Write the number of syllables you hear in front of each word. Draw lines where you divide the syllables in each word.

_____ **1.** comment   _____ **9.** southern   _____ **17.** trouble

_____ **2.** speechless   _____ **10.** caution   _____ **18.** although

_____ **3.** measles   _____ **11.** complaint   _____ **19.** athlete

_____ **4.** area   _____ **12.** surgery   _____ **20.** Styrofoam

_____ **5.** prowler   _____ **13.** loosen   _____ **21.** gymnasium

_____ **6.** assault   _____ **14.** awkward   _____ **22.** acceptable

_____ **7.** radio   _____ **15.** swallow   _____ **23.** disappointment

_____ **8.** poison   _____ **16.** purple   _____ **24.** Philadelphia

Lesson 11

LEARNING GOALS

Strategy: Predict what you might read about
Reading: Read a story
Skill: Understand character, setting, and plot
Writing: Write a story
Word Work: Summary of strategies for recognizing words

Before You Read

In "A Soldier's Story," a young man tells about being in the 1991 Persian Gulf War. The U.S. fought this war because the country of Iraq invaded its neighbor Kuwait. The U.S. wanted to force Iraq to withdraw from Kuwait. It also wanted to protect its supply of oil from Kuwait.

Before you read "A Soldier's Story," predict what a person writing about this war might describe. Check each thing you think you might read about.

_____ how it feels to go to war   _____ how it feels to be near death
_____ what it's like to fight   _____ what it's like to go home

List something else the soldier might tell about, or something you hope to read about.

_____

Key Words Read each sentence. Do you know the underlined words?
- <u>Negotiation</u> is better than war for solving problems.
- The <u>protective</u> suits would save the <u>soldiers</u> from a <u>chemical</u> attack.
- The only <u>communication</u> allowed was by hand signals.
- The sergeant heard a loud <u>explosion</u>.

▶ **Use the Strategy**

To help you understand "A Soldier's Story," keep guessing about what might happen next. Predict how the main character will act or feel.

A Soldier's Story

My name is Al Cruz. In 1991, I served my country in the Persian Gulf War. The United States went to the Persian Gulf for two reasons: to free Kuwait from Iraq and to protect our oil supply. The Gulf War lasted only 43 days, but it changed my beliefs forever. Before I fought in the Gulf, I believed that war was the only way to solve world problems. Now I believe the way to solve problems is through negotiation and compromise. This is what happened to change my mind.

It all started for me Saturday, February 23, at 20:00 army time. That was zero hour. If the Iraqis did not leave Kuwait by that time, we would begin a ground assault. The Iraqis didn't pull out. At 8:00 P.M. we began to move in.

The Iraqi soldiers had built walls of sand to fight behind. Our job as tank crewmen was to break through. Our tanks would cut wide openings in the sand walls. We wore protective suits and had gas masks in case of a chemical attack.

That night the desert was rainy and cold. The tanks moved through the darkness in long, narrow lines. We kept radio silence so the Iraqi soldiers would not detect us. Hand signals were our only communication.

My heart raced. After weeks of training and waiting, I was finally going into battle. I was on the front line. For the first time, my life was in danger.

Check-in ▶ What do you think will happen next?

Suddenly we heard an explosion. Then came two more quick blasts much closer to us. Then nothing. Inside the tank we stared at each other. Because of the radio blackout, we couldn't find out what had happened.

As our tank rolled on, our thoughts were all the same: Had one of our tanks been hit? Had people been killed? Were we going to be next?

Finally the message "mission accomplished" came over the radio. We returned to base. As I climbed out of the tank, I saw Sergeant Miles waiting. He broke the news. We had lost two tanks. The crewmen were dead. One of the men killed was Eddie, my best friend.

How do you think this news makes Al feel? How will he react?

◀ Check-in

When I heard the news, I leaned against a wall. A hundred thoughts went through my mind. Eddie and I had grown up together. We played basketball. Eddie had a wife and a baby. I had lost my best friend. Eddie was gone. He was the one person I could talk to about anything. I sat on the ground and cried. I hadn't cried for a long time.

Losing Eddie has helped me focus on what's important. Before the war, I didn't really value things like my kid's birthday or just hanging out with a friend. Now, I appreciate them more.

My buddies who didn't go to the Gulf give me a hard time when I talk like this. They say I've lost my edge. But they weren't there. They just don't know.

▶ **Final Check-in**
Did Al tell about the things you expected him to? Did any event surprise you? If so, what was it?

After You Read

A. **Did the Story Make Sense?** Reread sections you marked with a question mark (?). Do they make sense now? If not, discuss them with a partner or your instructor.

B. **Build Your Vocabulary** Look at the words you <u>underlined</u>. Can you figure them out now? If not, find out what they are. Add them to your word bank.

C. **Answer These Questions**

1. List the predictions you made in "Before You Read" on page 98 that were included in the story.

_____

_____

_____

2. Who is the soldier in the title "A Soldier's Story"?
  (1) Al Cruz
  (2) Eddie
  (3) Sergeant Miles

3. One effect of Eddie's death is that
  (1) the tank crew's mission was accomplished
  (2) Al Cruz decided what he thought about war
  (3) two tanks were lost

▶ **Talk About It**
Discuss the questions below with a partner or small group.
If you like, write a response.

Al expressed his feelings by writing this story. Do you think it helped him? In what ways?

Think About It: Understand Character, Setting, and Plot

You have learned that most stories have characters, a setting, and a plot.

- The **characters** are the people in the story. You learn about characters by reading and inferring about them.
- The **setting** is where and when the story takes place. The setting of a story can make you feel a certain way.
- The **plot** is the plan of action or series of events in a story. Most plots have three parts:

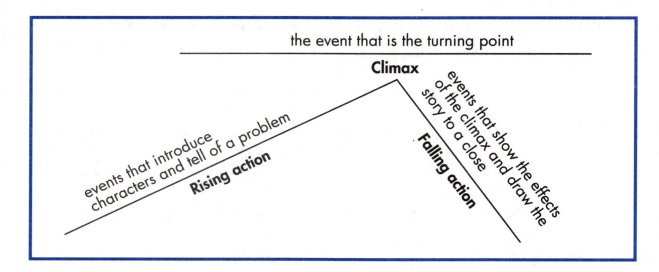

Practice   Answer these questions about "A Soldier's Story."

1. Name the characters in "A Soldier's Story." Write the main character first.

   _____   _____   _____

2. Check each term that helps describe Al Cruz.
   - _____ cared for Eddie   _____ cruel to others
   - _____ cowardly in battle   _____ lost his best friend
   - _____ changed his feelings   _____ values things more

3. Write one or two sentences to describe how you imagine Al Cruz looks.

   _____

   _____

4. Write about the setting.

    a. Where the story takes place _____

    b. When the story starts _____

5. Check each term that helps describe the setting.

_____ desert	_____ cold	_____ night	_____ peace	_____ tense
_____ rainy	_____ hot	_____ day	_____ war	_____ calm

6. Think about the plot in "A Soldier's Story." On the lines below, write "rising action," "climax," or "falling action" by each part of this story.

    a. Al and the rest of the tank crew move through the desert night. They hear explosions. They wonder what happened and if they will be next.

    This is the _____

    b. Al changes his mind about what he values.

    This is the _____

    c. Al is told that Eddie is dead. Al mourns.

    This is the _____

    Now complete a plot map for "A Soldier's Story."

Climax / Rising action / Falling action

Write About It: Write a Story

The war is over, and Al is back home. Write a story about what happens to him.

A. Prewrite Look at the pictures below of Al and his wife.
Decide which shows
(1) the rising action,
(2) the climax, and
(3) the falling action.
Number them.

Now fill in the plot map. Describe briefly what happens in each picture.

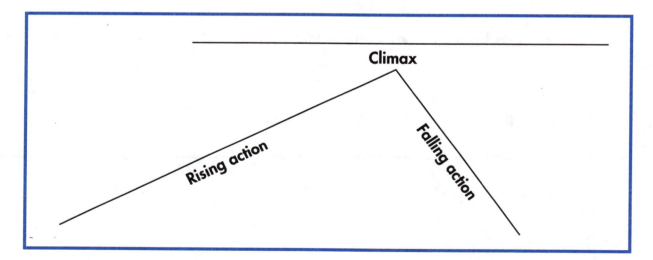

B. Write On another sheet of paper, write a story based on your plot map.

Read your story aloud. Then ask a classmate or friend to read his or her story out loud. How alike are the stories?

▶ **Hold on to this work.** You may use it again at this end of this unit.

Word Work: Summary of Strategies for Recognizing Words

You have learned about several strategies for recognizing unfamiliar words in your reading. They include:

- using context clues
- dividing long words into these smaller parts:
  - **a.** the smaller whole words in a compound word
  - **b.** prefixes, roots, and suffixes
  - **c.** syllables

When you are reading, you can combine the word division strategies with context clues to help you read with meaning.

Practice Read these words aloud. Draw lines where you divide the words. By each word, write the letter or letters of the strategies above that you used to divide the words. If you are unsure of the pronunciation or the meaning, look the word up in a dictionary.

_____ 1. themselves	_____ 11. professional	_____ 21. expectations
_____ 2. confusion	_____ 12. emergency	_____ 22. pronunciation
_____ 3. lineage	_____ 13. girlfriend	_____ 23. assurance
_____ 4. election	_____ 14. explosive	_____ 24. communication
_____ 5. relative	_____ 15. breakthrough	_____ 25. accomplishment
_____ 6. mistakenly	_____ 16. newspaper	_____ 26. qualification
_____ 7. grandchildren	_____ 17. predictable	_____ 27. amazement
_____ 8. expression	_____ 18. protection	_____ 28. hardheaded
_____ 9. offensive	_____ 19. authority	_____ 29. confidentially
_____ 10. separation	_____ 20. courtroom	_____ 30. dependability

▶ **Remember:** When you see an unfamiliar word, try to pronounce it. If you don't recognize it, say it another way. Keep trying until you hear a familiar word.

Lesson 12

LEARNING GOALS

Strategy: Use your experience to understand what you read
Reading: Read a poem
Skill: Make inferences
Writing: Write a letter

Before You Read

The poem "Arthur" was written by Susan Anderson. Susan wrote this poem in prison. In the poem, she expresses her feelings about being apart from someone she loves.

Have you ever been apart from someone you loved? Do you know someone who has? Think about people who are apart from their loved ones. Mark whether you believe each statement is **True** or **False.**

True	False	When people are separated from someone they love, they
_____	_____	feel content and calm
_____	_____	think about their happy memories with the other person
_____	_____	try to forget the person
_____	_____	feel alone and sad

Key Words Read each sentence. Do you know the underlined words?
- <u>Familiar</u> things feel safe and comfortable.
- The <u>absence</u> of a loved one can haunt a person.
- The meat of a deer is called <u>venison</u>.

▶ **Use the Strategy**

To help you understand the poem "Arthur," think about the poet's feelings. Think about your own experiences. Have you ever missed someone? Did you have any of the same feelings as the poet?

Arthur

Susan Anderson

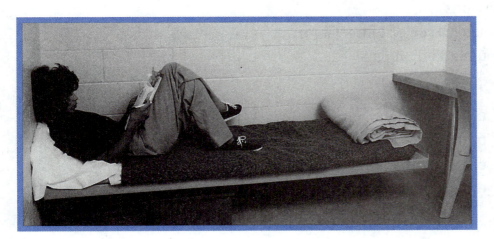

Familiar things haunt me,
With their absence from my life.

Grey blue eyes reach out to me.
Holding the promise of pain,
At my leaving.

So long now to wait
For the assurance of your touch.
Protected from the world,
In your strong safe embrace.

Only your voice on a cold plastic phone.
Through bullet proof glass,
Trying to memorize your face,
Until next week

Dreaming of passion I could be enjoying.
Thinking of that big walleye I got this spring,
And damning myself because there won't
Be any others this year
And no venison in the freezer.

▶ **Check-in**

As you read the poem, did you think about your own experiences of separation? How did they compare with the poet's?

After You Read

A. Did the Poem Make Sense? Reread sections you marked with a question mark (?). Do they make sense now? If not, discuss them with a partner or your instructor.

B. Build Your Vocabulary Look at the words you <u>underlined</u>. Can you figure them out now? If not, find out what they are. Add them to your word bank.

C. Answer These Questions

1. Mark these statements **True** or **False.** Compare your answers with the statements you marked on page 106.

True	False	The poet
_____	_____	**a.** feels content and calm
_____	_____	**b.** thinks about her happy memories with Arthur
_____	_____	**c.** is trying to forget Arthur
_____	_____	**d.** feels alone and sad

2. What do you think the theme of this poem is?
   (1) being protected from the world
   (2) being haunted by familiar things
   (3) the pain and loneliness of separation from someone you love

3. Which lines help you understand the theme?

   _____

   _____

   _____

 **Talk About It**

Discuss the questions below with a partner or small group. If you like, write a response.

Does the poet do a good job telling about her life and her feelings? Why or why not?

Think About It: Make Inferences

You can **infer** facts and ideas when you read. When you make inferences, you use clues to figure out something that isn't actually stated. For instance, the poet never tells us that the "you" in the poem is Arthur. We infer that from the title. What inference can you make from these lines?

▶ Familiar things haunt me,
With their absence from my life.

_____

You would probably infer that the poet is in an unfamiliar place and misses familiar things.

Now reread these lines from "Arthur."

▶ Only your voice on a cold plastic phone.
Through bullet proof glass,
Trying to memorize your face,
Until next week

Where are the poet and Arthur in this passage?

_____

You probably wrote, "They are in the visiting room of a prison." You can infer this because they are speaking over a phone through bulletproof glass.

Based on the poem, how often can the poet and Arthur see each other?

_____

You probably wrote "every week" or "once a week." You can infer this because the poet says she is trying to memorize Arthur's face "Until next week."

Practice Read these lines from "Arthur." Then check which inferences can be based on them.

A. ▶ Grey blue eyes reach out to me.
Holding the promise of pain,
At my leaving.

Yes	No	You can infer that
_____	_____	**1.** Arthur has grey blue eyes.
_____	_____	**2.** Arthur feels as deeply for the poet as she does for him.

B. ▶ So long now to wait
For the assurance of your touch.
Protected from the world,
In your strong safe embrace.

Yes	No	You can infer that
_____	_____	**3.** The poet will get out of prison very soon.
_____	_____	**4.** Arthur is a tall, heavy-set man.
_____	_____	**5.** Arthur made the poet feel safe.

C. ▶ Thinking of that big walleye I got this spring,
And damning myself because there won't
Be any others this year
And no venison in the freezer.

Yes	No	You can infer that
_____	_____	**6.** The poet enjoyed fishing and hunting.
_____	_____	**7.** The poet feels guilty for not being able to provide food for Arthur.

Write About It: Write a Letter

The poet of "Arthur" feels alone and sad. Suppose a friend of yours feels that way, and you want to help. Write a letter to your friend with some advice.

A. Prewrite Think of what advice you would give your friend. Write down a few ideas below. Share ideas with a partner. Write down some of your partner's ideas. Then choose the best ideas.

B. Write On your own paper, complete the letter below with the ideas and advice you would give your lonely friend.

Dear _____,

   It is never easy to be apart from someone you love. Two things that

might help you get through this time are _____

_____ and

_____

Think of people you can lean on, such as _____

_____

You might also _____

_____

_____

_____ I hope you will soon feel better.

Sincerely,

_____

          (your name)

▶ **Hold on to this work.** You may use it again at the end of this unit.

▶ Writing Skills Mini-Lesson: Fixing Sentence Fragments

A **sentence fragment** is an **incomplete thought.** It is important to write complete sentences, not sentence fragments. These are all sentence fragments:

- Can be fun to watch.
- Because sad movies make me cry.
- If my child asked to see a horror film.

If you find a fragment in your writing, you can fix it in two ways:

1. **You can fix some fragments by adding a subject or verb and other words to complete the thought.**
   - **Videos** can be fun to watch.

2. **If a fragment is a dependent clause standing alone, connect it to an independent clause.**
   - **I won't see that movie** because sad movies make me cry.
   - If my child asked to see a horror film, **I would say no.**

Practice On your own paper, rewrite each fragment as a complete sentence. Express your opinions about talk shows on TV.

1. I think TV talk shows.

I think TV talk shows are a waste of time.

I think TV talk shows are great.

2. I think talk-show hosts.

3. The guests often talk about.

4. When I watch a talk show.

5. I would like to see.

6. If I had the chance to be on a talk show.

Unit 4 Review

Reading Review

This reading is about expressing yourself. Read it and then answer the questions.

A Letter to the Editor

I have just learned that the public library will be forced to cut back on its hours due to funding cuts in next year's town budget. I've heard they may be cutting Saturday hours for one thing. This will be a real hardship for people like me.

I work full-time and am taking college courses at night. The only time I have to go to the library is Saturdays. If the library is closed on Saturdays, I don't know what I'll do. And what about people who like to take their children to the library on Saturdays? They will surely miss that.

The library is a vital community resource. As I understand it, if the funding is kept at current levels, about $12.50 would be added to the average homeowner's tax bill for next year. Isn't the library worth that?

I urge everyone who uses the library to contact their town council representative and ask that full funding for the library be restored to the budget.

Jo Ann Baker

1. What is the writer's main viewpoint?
    (1) The funding for the public library should not be cut.
    (2) The town should stop funding the public library.
    (3) Everybody uses the public library.

2. Does anything about the writer help explain his viewpoint? _____

    If yes, what? _____

3. Can you infer these ideas from the letter?

    Yes   **No**
    _____ _____ **a.** The writer isn't doing well in college.
    _____ _____ **b.** The writer doesn't have a lot of free time.

Writing Process

In Unit 4, you wrote three first drafts. Choose the piece that you would like to work with more. You will revise, edit, and make a final copy of this draft.

    _____ your review of something you have seen or read (page 96)
    _____ your story about what happens to Al Cruz (page 104)
    _____ your letter to a friend who is lonely (page 111)

Find the first draft you chose. Then turn to page 128 in this book. Follow steps 3, 4, and 5 in the Writing Process to create a final draft.

As you revise, check your draft for this specific point:

Review: Did you include both good and bad points?

Story: Did you follow the plot sequence: rising action, climax, falling action?

Letter: Have you included clear details on what someone who is alone and sad might do?

Skills Review

This Skills Review will let you see how well you can use the skills taught in this book. When you have completed Units 1–4, do this review. Then share your work with your instructor.

Reading Skills Review

Read each passage and answer the questions that follow.

Grandma Moses

Age should not limit a person. That statement was proved by a woman called Grandma Moses. Grandma Moses was born Anna Mary Robertson in New York State in 1860. When Anna was 27, she married Thomas Salmon Moses. Anna spent much of her life on farms in northern New York. She was a hardworking farm wife. When she had a little time to relax, she did needlework.

When Anna was in her 70s, a joint disease made it difficult for her to hold sewing needles. But Anna discovered that she could still hold paintbrushes. She had never had an art lesson in her life, but she began to paint. Anna painted simple but lively and brightly colored pictures of life in the country. Her paintings were inspired by memories of her youth.

An art collector discovered Anna's paintings in the 1930s. Art reviewers began to praise her work. They called it fresh and new and charming. Because of Anna's age, people started calling her Grandma Moses. Grandma Moses painted for more than 20 years. She died when she was 101. But she proved that you are never too old to find new ways to express yourself.

Choose the best answer for each question.

1. What is the main idea of this short biography?
   (1) Grandma Moses's real name was Anna Mary Robertson.
   (2) A joint disease made Grandma Moses give up needlework.
   (3) Grandma Moses proved you are never too old to start something new.

2. Which of the following details supports the main idea?
   (1) Grandma Moses was born Anna Mary Robertson.
   (2) Grandma Moses started painting after she was 70.
   (3) Grandma Moses lived past 100.

3. Which of the following can you infer about Grandma Moses' paintings?
   (1) They were unlike most paintings done at the time.
   (2) They were praised only because she was old.
   (3) They showed how hard life was in the country.

The New Shop

Marcus was sitting alone in the new shop. He looked out at the busy street. Why wasn't anybody coming in? Marcus remembered how excited he and his friends were when they first got the idea for the shop. James, Les, and he were trying to earn money. It was James who first thought about a sandwich shop and bakery.

"Les, you're a great cook, and your wife is the best baker I know. This neighborhood needs a place to buy good, quick food. The factory has reopened. The workers want a decent place to buy lunch. Many would probably stop for breakfast, too."

So James had thought of the idea, and his uncle had lent him some money to start the business. Les and his wife were the cook and baker. Marcus's job was to sell the food. But he hadn't been able to do that.

Marcus kept watching the people pass by. Not one noticed the "Grand Opening" signs in the window. Then he saw some boys playing on the corner. Suddenly Marcus got an idea. If people would not come to their food, he would bring the food to the people.

"Hey, kids, come here for a minute," he called to two boys. Marcus promised the boys all they could eat. But they had to eat their sandwiches and baked goods on the corner. And they had to talk loudly about how good the food was and where it came from.

Marcus's idea worked. Within half an hour, the shop had its first customer. Within a week, the friends' dream of owning their own shop began to come true.

Choose the best answer for each question.

4. What is Marcus's problem in this story?
    (1) getting people to come into a shop
    (2) getting the factory to reopen
    (3) keeping boys away from his shop

5. Which term best describes Marcus?
    (1) lazy
    (2) clever
    (3) unsure

6. The setting of this story is a shop in
    (1) the country
    (2) a factory
    (3) a city neighborhood

Writing Skills Review

Edit the paragraph. Correct any mistakes you find in compound and complex sentences. Fix sentence fragments. Use commas correctly.

Alderman Ramon Mendez is known as a man who gets the job done. Mendez represents. A largely Latino neighborhood. Before Mendez was elected four years ago this neighborhood got poor service from the city. Garbage pickup was not steady and potholes pitted the streets. Police patrols were few and far between. However, Mendez changed that. He began to speak up, as soon as he became alderman. He said that his neighborhood had waited too long. It was time for the city. To give equal service to all areas. Now services have improved greatly. Although there are still some problems. The neighborhood is cleaner and safer. Mendez is proud of his work.

Write About It

On a separate piece of paper, write about the topic below. Follow steps 1–3 of the Writing Process on page 128 to write and revise your draft. Then give your draft to your instructor for some feedback.

Topic: What do you think is the most important thing a parent can teach his or her child? Explain why you think so.

Skills Review Answers

Reading Skills Review

1. (3)   4. (1)
2. (2)   5. (2)
3. (1)   6. (3)

Writing Skills Review

Alderman Ramon Mendez is known as a man who gets the job done. Mendez represents a largely Latino neighborhood. Before Mendez was elected four years ago, this neighborhood got poor service from the city. Garbage pickup was not steady, and potholes pitted the streets. Police patrols were few and far between. However, Mendez changed that. He began to speak up as soon as he became alderman. He said that his neighborhood had waited too long. It was time for the city to give equal service to all areas. Now services have improved greatly. Although there are still some problems, the neighborhood is cleaner and safer. Mendez is proud of his work.

Write About It

Write a final draft using steps 4 and 5 of the Writing Process. Share your final draft with your instructor.

Evaluation Chart

Check your Review answers. Then circle the number of any answer you missed. You may need to review the lessons indicated next to that question number.

Question	Skill	Lessons
1	find the main idea	3, 8
2	find supporting details	3, 8
3	draw conclusions, infer	5, 12,
4	understand plot	2, 12
5	understand character	6, 11
6	identify setting	7, 8

Now go back and fill in the right side of the Student Interest Inventory on pages 6 and 7.

▶ Answer Key

▼ Lesson 1

After You Read (p. 14)
Sample answers:
C. 1. a. food
     b. rest or relax
     c. housing or shelter
  2. (1)
  3. start a free food program for children and open a shelter for the homeless

Think About It: Find the Theme (p. 15)
Practice
A. 1. homeless people
  2. (2)
B. 3. hunger
  4. (3)

▼ Lesson 2

After You Read (p. 21)
Sample answers:
C. 1. a. Kim Washington and Todd Walker
     b. an auto assembly line
     c. Todd does not think Kim is qualified to be the boss.
     d. Kim responds to Todd, and everyone goes back to work.
  2. (1)
  3. (2)

Think About It: Understand the Plot (p. 22)
Practice
Sample answers follow. Your answers may be shorter, but they should say about the same thing:
1. **Rising action:** Todd and Bill start to argue. They push each other.
  Climax: Workers move in and break up the fight.
  Falling action: The workers don't want any more trouble. Everyone goes back to work.
2. **Rising action:** Todd sees a worker doing something dangerous, tries to warn him, but is not heard.

Climax: Todd shuts down the line.
Falling action: Kim hurries over, listens to Todd's explanation, and thanks him.

Word Work: Using Context Clues to Figure Out Word Meaning (p. 25)
Practice
1. (1)
2. (2)
3. (2)

▼ Lesson 3

After You Read (p. 29)
Sample answers:
C. 1. a. bad, tense, not confident
     b. happy, proud
  2. Any one of these answers: He learned discipline *or* He turned his game around in college *or* He was NBA Rookie of the Year.
  3. (1)

Think About It: Find the Main Idea and Details (p. 30)
Practice
1. **Details:** tempted by drugs; cannot handle the pressure of playing before people
2. **Main Idea:** Parents often have high expectations for their children.
Details: to be honest and follow the rules; to get along with others; to do their best; to be what the parents wanted to be

Word Work: Recognizing Words (p. 33)
Practice
1. under stand
2. after noon
3. class room
4. thumb nail
5. every where

▼ Writing Skills Mini-Lesson: Compound Sentences (p. 34)
There are different ways to complete the sentences. Here are some sample answers. Check your sentences with your instructor.
1. I want to get a better job, so **I am going back to school.**
2. **I need to improve my skills,** so I will study hard.

3. It may be difficult, but **I will do it.**
4. **I want to be a nurse,** and I will work to meet this goal.
5. I will **meet my goals**, or I will **set new ones.**

▼ **Unit 1 Review (p. 35)**
1. (2)
2. (2)
3. (3)

Unit 2 Across Generations

▼ **Lesson 4**

After You Read (p. 40)
C. 1. There are many possible answers. Check your answer with your instructor.
2. sturdy, able, powerful, full of energy
3. (1)

Think About It: Find the Theme (p. 41)
Practice
A. 1. grandparents
2. grandparents being links to the past
B. 3. single fathers
4. a single father realizing that he is not alone

▼ **Lesson 5**

After You Read (p. 47)
C. 1. There are many possible answers. Check your answer with your instructor.
2. a. Possible answers:
     Tina and Kevin got married eight months ago.
     They have been together three years.
     Almost one year ago, Tina went to a program for people with an addiction to alcohol.
     Tina tried to hide her drinking from her husband.
     He confronted Tina about her drinking.
   b. Possible answers:
     Tina and her husband will work hard to make their marriage work.
     Tina hopes to remain sober.
     She wants to be a responsible mother.
     Tina wants to find a job.
     She can't wait to hold her baby.
3. (1)

Think About It: Draw Conclusions (p. 48)
Practice
A. 1. Yes, because she knows her baby is a boy.
2. No
B. 3. Yes, because he did not know she had a problem until they moved in together.
4. Yes, because he stayed with Tina and helped her confront her drinking problem.
C. 5. Yes, because she says "work again" and "back to work."
6. No

Word Work: Prefixes and Roots (p. 51)
Practice
A. 1. pre/dict   7. pre/view
2. anti/freeze   8. trans/late
3. mis/take   9. mis/chief
4. trans/form   10. anti/biotic
5. pre/fix   11. mis/lead
6. anti/slavery   12. trans/pire
B. Some possible answers:

deduce	inspect	reduce	subscribe
deform	inscribe	reform	transact
describe	permit	remit	transform
induce	perform	respect	transmit
inform	react	submit	transcribe

▼ **Lesson 6**

After You Read (p. 55)
C. 1. a. he saw Officer Wade was nervous.
     b. he realized Brian had been arrested.
     c. Brian did not talk or look at him.
2. (1)
3. (2)

Think About It: Understand Character (p. 56)
Practice
A. 1. True
2. True
B. 3. False
4. False

Word Work: Prefixes, Roots, and Suffixes (p. 59)
Practice
A. 1. in/vent/or   5. ad/vantage/ous
2. out/rage/ous   6. con/tract/or
3. dis/cuss/ion   7. react/ion
4. de/pend/able   8. trans/port/able

B. Some possible words:

expect	expression	reportable
expectation	inspect	repress
export	inspection	repression
exportable	portable	respect
express	report	respectable

▼ Writing Skills Mini-Lesson: Complex Sentences (p. 60)

There are many possible answers. Here are some samples. Check your sentences with your instructor.

1. **My parents worked** while I was at school.
2. **My mother lived in Tennessee** when she was young.
3. **My father found a job** before I was born.
4. **My parents separated** after I was born.
5. **My mother stayed at home** when I was a baby.
6. **My father lived on a farm** when he was growing up.
7. **My father spent time with me** while I was growing up.
8. **My parents got along better** after they got older.

▼ Unit 2 Review (p. 61)

1. (3)
2. (1)
3. Yes, because he thinks about his son and then decides to work harder at his marriage.

Unit 3 Voices for Justice

▼ Lesson 7

After You Read (p. 67)

C. 1. There are many possible answers. Discuss your answer with a partner or your instructor.
 2. (2)
 3. Jane comes to Clara's House. Clara tells Jane she can choose to stay. Mick calls Jane. Jane decides to stay.

Think About It: Identify Setting (p. 68)
Practice

A. 1. the front room at Clara's House
 2. (2)

B. 3. a hospital emergency room on a Saturday night
 4. (1)
 5. Possible answers: doors flew open; gunshot victim rushed in on a stretcher; shot; doctor tore open the victim's shirt; face was grim; began to work quickly; knew the man might not live

Word Work: Dividing Words into Syllables (p. 71)
Practice

2	1. wea/ry	3	13. vi/o/lence
2	2. a/void	2	14. moun/tain
2	3. greed/y	2	15. coc/oon
1	4. throat	2	16. cous/in
3	5. ra/di/o	2	17. drows/y
2	6. rea/son	2	18. law/yer
2	7. sham/poo	4	19. cer/e/mo/ny
2	8. be/tween	3	20. au/di/ence
2	9. thou/sand	3	21. main/te/nance
2	10. part/ner	2	22. al/though
2	11. fur/nish	4	23. co/or/di/nate
2	12. re/straint	4	24. ex/pe/ri/ence

▼ Lesson 8

After You Read (p. 76)

C. 1. Sample answer: Apartheid was unjust because blacks had almost no rights.
 2. (2)
 3. (1)

Think About It: Understand the Main Idea and Details (p. 77)
Practice

A Young Leader: led nonviolent protests for justice; began to sabotage

A Famous Prisoner: sentenced to life in prison at 45; worked to improve inmate conditions

President of a Nation: was elected president in 1994; promised to work for all races

Word Work: More Dividing Words into Syllables (p. 79)
Practice

2	1. mar/ble	2	6. sud/den
2	2. sur/prise	2	7. dis/trict
2	3. bub/ble	2	8. cof/fee
2	4. knowl/edge	2	9. hud/dle
3	5. al/pha/bet	3	10. friend/li/er

_2_ 11. hard/ly	_3_ 24. flam/ma/ble	
_2_ 12. win/ner	_2_ 25. sprin/kle	
_2_ 13. mid/dle	_2_ 26. set/ting	
_3_ 14. ath/let/ic	_3_ 27. un/sta/ble	
_2_ 15. hun/dred	_3_ 28. sup/pli/er	
_2_ 16. ad/dress	_2_ 29. laugh/ter	
_2_ 17. can/dle	_3_ 30. pos/si/ble	
_2_ 18. pan/try	_2_ 31. grid/dle	
_2_ 19. bet/ter	_4_ 32. trans/for/ma/tion	
_2_ 20. pump/kin	_3_ 33. dif/fer/ence	
_3_ 21. de/part/ment	_2_ 34. wrin/kle	
_3_ 22. pret/ti/er	_3_ 35. mer/chan/dise	
_2_ 23. trou/ble	_3_ 36. dis/ap/pear	

▼ Lesson 9

After You Read (p. 82)

C. 1. (3)
   2. (3)
   3. free to choose my own teachers

Think About It: Identify Viewpoint (p. 83)

Practice

1. (1)
2. (2)
3. (2)

▼ Writing Skills Mini-Lesson: More on Complex Sentences (p. 86)

2. Although some parents were silent, most parents spoke out.
   Most parents spoke out although some parents were silent.
3. Because the families protested, the school reopened.
   The school reopened because the families protested.
4. If a school closes, the children lose.
   The children lose if a school closes.
5. Because they enjoyed school, the children did well. The children did well because they enjoyed school.
6. Although it needed repairs, the school was reopened. The school was reopened although it needed repairs.
7. If they work together, parents can get things done. Parents can get things done if they work together.

8. Since the parents helped, the repairs were quickly made. The repairs were quickly made since the parents helped.

▼ Unit 3 Review (p. 87)

1. (2)
2. is a good lawyer; works long hours; acts as a social worker
3. False

Unit 4 Express Yourself

▼ Lesson 10

After You Read (p. 93)

C. 1. Sample answers follow. Any two:
      what day the show is on
      what time the show is on
      what the show is about
      the reviewer's opinion of the show
   2. False
   3. False

Think About It: Identify Viewpoint (p. 94)

Practice

1. a. Positive. Possible answers: "Anyone who loves music would have loved this show." "best moments," "Hearing her voice is a wonderful experience."
   b. Yes. He is a music teacher.
2. a. Positive. Possible answers: "The show was excellent." "gave me a close-up view of what happened to an important person," "I was impressed."
   b. Yes. He is a student who is learning about a topic discussed in the show.
3. a. Negative. Possible answers: "I didn't think the show was very good." "not enough to make me enjoy watching the show"
   b. Yes. She doesn't like that kind of music.

Word Work: Review of Dividing Words into Syllables (p. 97)
Practice

2	1. com ment		2	13. loos en
2	2. speech less		2	14. awk ward
2	3. mea sles		2	15. swal low
3	4. ar e a		2	16. pur ple
2	5. prowl er		2	17. trou ble
2	6. as sault		2	18. al though
3	7. ra di o		2	19. ath lete
2	8. poi son		3	20. Sty ro foam
2	9. south ern		4	21. gym na si um
2	10. cau tion		4	22. ac cep ta ble
2	11. com plaint		4	23. dis ap point ment
3	12. sur ger y		5	24. Phil a del phi a

▼ Lesson 11

After You Read (p. 101)
C. 1. There are many possible answers. Check your answers with your instructor.
2. (1)
3. (2)

Think About It: Understand Character, Setting, and Plot (p. 102)
Practice
1. Al Cruz, Sergeant Miles, Eddie
2. cared for Eddie, values things more, changed his feelings, lost his best friend
3. Answers will vary.
4. a. the Persian Gulf
   b. February 23, 1991
5. desert, rainy, cold, night, war, tense
6. a. rising action
   b. falling action
   c. climax

Word Work: Summary of Strategies for Recognizing Words (p. 105)
Practice
Strategies may vary. Some words can be divided one way by prefix, root, and suffix and another way by syllables. Any division that will help you to recognize the word is OK.

▼ Lesson 12

After You Read (p. 108)
C. 1. a. False
   b. True
   c. False
   d. True
2. (3)
3. Sample answers: "Familiar things haunt me"; "The promise of pain at my leaving"; "So long now to wait"; "Trying to memorize your face until next week"; "Dreaming of passion I could be enjoying"; "Damning myself"

Think About It: Make Inferences (p. 109)
Practice
A. 1. Yes
   2. Yes
B. 3. No
   4. No
   5. Yes
C. 6. Yes
   7. Yes

▼ Writing Skills Mini-Lesson: Fixing Sentence Fragments (p. 112)
There are many possible answers. Here are some samples. Check your sentences with your instructor.
2. I think talk-show hosts are only concerned about ratings.
   I think talk-show hosts can be very funny.
3. The guests often talk about disgusting things.
   The guests often talk about important things.
4. When I watch a talk show, I get bored.
   When I watch a talk show, I learn about life.
5. I would like to see fewer talk shows on TV.
   I would like to see more stars on talk shows.
6. If I had the chance to be on a talk show, I wouldn't do it.
   If I had the chance to be on a talk show, I would be excited.

▼ Unit 4 Review (p. 113)
1. (1)
2. Yes. If the library funding is not cut, the library will remain open on Saturdays when she can use it.
3. a. No
   b. Yes

Writing Skills

This Handbook lists the rules you learned in the Writing Skills Mini-Lessons in this book.

Compound Sentences

A **compound sentence** has two or more complete thoughts joined by a connecting word such as *and, but, so,* or *or.* To write a compound sentence, follow these rules.

1. **Make each part of the sentence a *complete thought*.** In each part, include a **subject** (who or what the sentence is about) and a **verb** (what the subject does or is).

    S V   S   V
    - **I have** a plan for my future, and **nobody will stop** me.

2. **Use the correct connecting word.** Use a *comma* before the connecting word.
    - *and* for related words
    - *but* for contrasting ideas
    - *so* for one idea that causes another
    - *or* for two choices

    My sons are now in school, **so** I have more time to study.

Fixing Sentence Fragments

A **sentence fragment** is an **incomplete thought.** These are sentence fragments:

- Can be fun to watch.
- Because sad movies make me cry.

If you find a fragment in your writing, you can fix it in two ways:

1. You can fix some fragments by adding a subject or verb and other words to complete the thought:
    TV can be fun to watch.

2. If a fragment is a dependent clause standing alone, you can connect it to an independent clause:
    Because sad movies make me cry, **I won't see that movie.**

Complex Sentences

A **complex sentence** has two parts: an independent clause and a dependent clause. A **clause** is a group of words containing a **subject** and a **verb**. This is a complex sentence:

- My parents were very young when they met.

1. **An independent clause is a complete thought. It can stand alone as a simple sentence.**

   Independent clause: My parents were very young.

2. **A dependent clause is an incomplete thought. It can start with a time word like *when, while, before,* or *after*. A dependent clause cannot stand alone.**

   Dependent clause: when they met

3. Be sure to include a subject and a verb in each clause.

   - **My parents were** very young when **they met.**

4. The dependent clause can come first or last in a complex sentence. If you put it first, use a comma between the clauses. If you put the dependent clause at the end of a sentence, don't use a comma.

   - **When the school closed,** the parents protested.
   - The parents protested **when the school closed.**

5. You can use words like *because, although, if,* and *since* in the dependent clause to show how the two thoughts in the sentence are related.

   - The students did well **because** the teachers cared.
   - **Although** the school was small, it had a fine library.
   - **If** parents get involved, they can make a difference.

The Writing Process

The Writing Process is a series of stages that can help you create a good piece of writing. These stages are shown below.

1. Prewrite, or plan your writing.

A. Think about your topic.

B. List ideas about your topic.

C. Organize your ideas.
  - Decide which ideas you will use.
  - Decide how you will order them.

2. Write a first draft.

A. Use your ideas from stage 1.

B. Write about your topic.
  - Include your most important ideas.
  - Use details to explain what you mean.

3. Revise your first draft.

A. Check that your draft

____ includes your important ideas

____ has details to explain what you mean

____ is clear and easy to understand

B. Make changes to improve your writing.

4. Edit your work.

A. Check your draft for errors in

____ spelling

____ punctuation

____ capitalization

____ complete sentences

B. Correct any mistakes you find. If you need help, use the Writing Skills Handbook on page 126 or ask your instructor.

5. Recopy your draft.

A. Write a final draft. Include your revising and editing changes.

B. Compare your first and final drafts. Note improvements.

C. Share your final draft with a classmate, a friend, or your instructor.